THE ORIENT PEARLS

THE ORIENT PEARLS

INDIAN FOLK-LORE

SHOVONA DEVI

GYAN

Published by

Gyan Publishing House
5, Ansari Road
Daryaganj, New Delhi-110002
Phone: 011-47034999, 9811692060
E-mail: books@gyanbooks.com

Distribution Network
gyanbooks.com
India, USA, Canada, UK, Australia, France

ISBN: 978-81-212-9126-2 (PB)
First Published, 1915

2nd Impression 2023

Printed at: Gyan Press, Delhi.

THE ORIENT PEARLS
AUTHOR: SHOVONA DEVI

THE ORIENT PEARLS

Photo Bourne & Shepherd

THE ORIENT PEARLS

INDIAN FOLK-LORE

BY

SHOVONA DEVI

MACMILLAN AND CO., LIMITED
ST. MARTIN'S STREET, LONDON
1915

PREFATORY NOTE

THE idea of writing these tales occurred to me while reading a volume of short stories by my uncle, Sir Rabindranath Tagore; but as I have none of his inventive genius, I set about collecting folk-tales and putting them into an English garb; and the tales contained in the following pages were told to me by various illiterate village folks, and not a few by a blind man still in my service, with a retentive memory, and a great capacity for telling a story.

SHOVONA DEVI.

CONTENTS

CONTENTS

THE ORIENT PEARLS.

A FEAST OF FISTS.

ONCE upon a time there lived a young Brahmin and his wife in what would, judged even by the standard of asceticism of their class, be deemed extreme poverty. Dragging along a sort of dead-and-alive existence upon scanty and miserable fare, they were too proud to beg or borrow, and too honest to steal.

Yet, for all this, their faith in Providence never wavered, but, on the other hand, they discerned in their present distress its iron hand forging for them a closely veiled destiny through its ever mysterious ways.

Fortified in this belief, they bore with philosophy their adversity until the gloom thickened around them, unrelieved, as it seemed to them, by a single redeeming gleam of hope.

One day, maddened by the sight of his starving wife (for to such straits had they been reduced) the young Brahmin set out towards the forest in search of wild roots and fruits for her, but alas! no sooner had he got there than he found the forest on fire and its denizens, terror-stricken, fleeing away in all directions.

Thus disappointed, he sat down at the foot of an ancient banyan-tree, under which a whole army might well have bivouacked, and began to pour forth his woes to the four winds of heaven in loud cries and lamentations after the fashion of all Orientals.

As the shades of evening fell, Haro and Gouri, guardian deities and succourers of humanity in distress, happened to be walking the earth, and his cries and lamentations reached their ears. "Hark, lord!" said Gouri, addressing her spouse, "Is not that the cry of some mortal lamenting his lot? He must be in sore distress. Let us go and relieve him."

Haro, annoyed at the idea of his walk being cut short, tried to dissuade her, saying: "Fair goddess! suffering is the badge of mankind. Indeed, these mortals bring down suffering upon their own heads by sheer demerit, and suffer they must, do all you can, until they have passed through the usual cycles of birth, death, and re-birth, again and again, working out demerit by merit in the process, and thus paving the way for final absorption into the Deity, the source of their being. So why trouble about these wretches?"

The goddess, whose feminine heart refused to be convinced by his male logic, insisted upon Haro accompanying her to the spot whence the cry arose, and Haro was obliged to give in to his headstrong spouse.

As soon as the Brahmin saw Haro and Gouri, whom he recognized by the halo around their heads, coming towards him, he set up a still louder wailing as if to move them, specially the goddess, to pity.

> They asked him what his mind oppressed,
> What woe lodged in his priestly breast.

The youth then told Haro and Gouri, between sobs and tears, of the domestic tragedy enacted from day to day—of the starving of his young wife and himself—and pointed, in corroboration, to his ribs, which were almost visible in his emaciated frame—a sight and a tale which could not but tell even upon the most callous of gods.

> The tale their hearts to pity moved—
> A magic cup the gods approved,
> A cup so bounteous, so designed,
> As could, at once, feed all mankind.

Haro then presented the Brahmin with the magic cup which, he took pains to assure him, had the miraculous power of producing toothsome dainties of any kind and in any quantity whatsoever for the mere asking.

Overjoyed with his present, the Brahmin thanked his divine benefactors in Oriental hyperbole, and no sooner were their backs turned upon him than he put the cup at once to the test—and lo and behold ! true to the word of the gods, there began to flow, in a continuous stream, delicacy after delicacy, such as had never been tasted by mortal lips before, and the Brahmin ate and ate until he could eat no more. Then, taking the cup up in his hand, and carefully wrapping the remainder of the food in the folds of his turban, he turned his steps homeward.

On the way, however, while passing by a cottage, he heard some little children crying for more bread and milk than their poor parents could give them. He walked in, and generously offered the children as much bread and milk as they desired out of the magic cup, and while he was watching them eat and drink, and talking with their parents, the cup was secretly removed, and another substituted in its place, which was in no way distinguishable from it except by the eyes of gods.

After the children had made a good meal and quieted

down, the Brahmin got up and, amidst the vociferous thanks of their parents, took his leave.

He now hurried home, and, arriving late at night, as he had to walk a long distance across the fields, found his wife sitting up anxiously waiting for him. As soon as she caught sight of her husband, she rushed forward to receive what he had brought, and, seeing a cup in his hand, fancied it contained something for her to eat. She seized the cup with eagerness, for she had not broken her fast that day, but, finding it empty, threw it straight away. The Brahmin, however, immediately rushed up and caught it before it could touch the ground.

"What a silly thing you have done!" said the Brahmin to his wife in a tone of rebuke. "You have desecrated the gift of the gods." Having told her all about the cup, and how and where and from whom he had received it, he said, "Do not fancy the cup is empty! Ask of it whatever you wish to eat, and that you will have at once, and in any quantity."

"I am dying of hunger," replied the wife in a tone of penitence. "I do not hanker after delicacies, but a little of the coarse fare I am used to will quite content me."

As she said this, she wept and repented of her sacrilege in contemptuously throwing away a sacred gift—of her folly in attempting to kill, as it were, the goose that was to lay golden eggs for the rest of their mortal lives.

However, being extremely hungry, she was going to ask the cup for her usual fare, when her husband interposed and pressed her to ask of it some tempting morsel; so she asked for this, that, and a dozen other delicacies all at once, but alas! nothing, absolutely nothing, came out of the cup. They quite thought that her desecration of the cup had caused its magic to vanish, and, at a loss what to do, they looked into it carefully, and turned it up and down several times; but not a morsel of food such as would satisfy the smallest of small microbes could they find in it. So the woman, handing it back to her husband, instead of dashing it to the ground as she had half a mind to do, sat down and began to weep, for she felt keenly her husband's cruelty in playing what she fancied was a practical joke while she was almost dying of starvation.

The Brahmin, amazed beyond measure at the failure of the divine cup to produce food, began to examine it carefully, as if there were some flaw which prevented the magic working; but he failed to discover any, and then put all the blame upon his wife, for had she not desecrated the cup? However, "It's no use crying over spilt milk," he thought, and, seeing his wife actually starving, and suddenly remembering the remains of his recent meal in the folds of his turban, he gave them to her to eat.

"Have you broken your fast, dear?" she asked him, ashamed of her conduct in desiring to satisfy her hunger before her lord had eaten. "How selfish I am!" said she. "I will not eat a morsel of this food unless you share it with me." And it was only when he had sworn to her a hundred times that he had already attended to his own wants that she could be persuaded to partake of some.

The next day the Brahmin youth again repaired to the foot of the same banyan-tree, and began to rend the air with still louder cries and lamentations than he had raised the evening before.

At night-fall Haro and Gouri were again taking their evening walk on earth, and his cries and lamentations, loud enough to rend the heavens in twain, reached their ears. "Hark, lord! hark!" said Gouri to her spouse, "another mortal seems to be in distress. Can you not do something for him too?"

Haro saw the prospect of another evening being spoilt, but, finding it impossible to dissuade his headstrong consort, he accompanied her to the foot of the banyan-tree, where the Brahmin had stationed himself. As the latter saw them approaching, he set up a still louder wailing, as if desirous of enlisting their sympathy by the strength of his cries rather than by the actual measure of his distress; for, Brahmin as he was, he had a shrewd insight into the mind of the gods.

Gouri, moved to pity by his cries, and failing to recognize him in the twilight, enquired the reason of his tears, and the Brahmin repeated, between his sobs (the characteristics of all beggars) the same story as on the previous evening.

Haro walked up close to the man, and, after rubbing his eyes and scanning the man's features well, said: "You silly man! what have you done with the magic cup we gave you only last evening? You have sold it, have you not, and come again for another? You are a dishonest rogue."

The Brahmin, taking the dust off the toes of the god, powdered his hair, or rather the top-knot of his order, and, with folded arms, protested his innocence. "I do not know, my lord," said he, "what thou art pleased to call a magic cup; both my wife and I tried it, but it conceived nothing and brought forth nothing, and my wife had to go to bed hungry. I did, indeed, find something in it at the time you presented it to me, but perhaps that was previously put there, and not produced by magic."

Now it was Haro's turn to protest that he had practised no fraud upon him, and that his cup still possessed the same miraculously productive power as before. Nevertheless, determined to prove their good faith to the Brahmin, Haro and Gouri requested him to take them to his hut and show them the cup.

The Brahmin, feeling sure his divine guests would be able to produce enough food for him and his wife as well as for themselves out of the cup, readily took them to his humble cottage; but the way was long, and Haro and Gouri soon began to feel tired and hungry, for it was close upon dinner-time for the gods, and conches and bells were sounding in the temples round.

As soon as they arrived with the Brahmin at his hut, the Brahmini knew at once by the halo round their heads who her guests were, and was at a loss how to entertain them. However, shrewd, practical woman as she was, she had bartered away the useless cup for a little useful rice, and had cooked some nice curry to eat with it, and was expecting her husband to bring her another, which she intended to deal with in the same way next day.

The Brahmini washed the feet of her divine guests, and then, placing the savoury rice and curry on two broad leaves in front of them, begged them to partake of the meal; but Haro and Gouri, although their mouths were watering, refused to eat the food, owing, as they put it, to caste scruples. The gods, they said, were of superior caste to mortals; but the Brahmini easily rose to the occasion, and her feminine wit supplied her with a crushing answer to them. She coolly assured her guests that the origin of herself and her husband was as divine as they themselves claimed, for all Brahmins, she reminded them with a smile of superior wisdom, were the offspring of Brahma, the Sirdar of the gods. Putting into the hands of Haro a copy of the sacred writings, she asked him to refresh his memory.

Haro and Gouri felt quite abashed, and, without another word, fell to, and between them did full justice to the curry and rice, for with the long tramp across the country their appetites had grown keen. Nothing was left, as you may well imagine, for their host and hostess, save the usual "prasad," or sacred leavings.

After the entertainment, Haro asked the Brahmin to produce his cup, and the latter in his turn asked his wife to fetch it. With consternation she confessed that she had bartered it for a little rice with a neighbour, but offered to produce it presently. So saying, she went out and brought it back in a few minutes.

"You said you never sold the cup," said Haro, turning to the Brahmin. "What does your wife say then?"

"She must have done that after I had left home," replied the Brahmin, apologetically, "and because she had found the cup quite useless as a food-producer." Needless to say, Haro was not satisfied with this explanation; nevertheless, he took the cup in his hand to see what was wrong with it. He saw at once that it was not the cup that he had given to the Brahmin, but quite a different one; the difference, however, was indistinguishable to any eye but that of the god.

He cross-examined the Brahmin as cleverly as a lawyer, as to his previous day's movements, and had little difficulty in the end in discovering the reason why the cup had apparently lost its virtue, for the one before him was a counterfeit.

Haro gave the Brahmin another cup, saying, "You are a silly man! You did not take good care of your cup, which must have been secretly exchanged for the one you showed me. Take this to the house of your friends, for whose children you so generously produced bread and milk yesterday, and see what follows." Thereupon Haro and Gouri took leave of their host and hostess.

The Brahmin, obeying the orders of the god, went to the house of these people just at the time when they were invoking the stolen cup for their dinner; as they saw him coming, they hid the cup, and, welcoming him with outward courtesy, asked him to be seated. Seeing another cup in his hand, they now thought of robbing him of this too.

The Brahmin, guessing their thoughts, said, "Is there any nice thing you would like to eat? Just open the lid of this cup, and out it will come."

Then these wicked people, taking the Brahmin at his word, opened the lid, when, horror of horrors! out flew from within it fists innumerable, which dealt them blows on their necks, noses, and ears, and beat them black and blue.

They cried out to the Brahmin to call back his fists into the cup, and, fetching the one they had stolen out of its hiding-place, and handing it over to him, prayed him to be gone with all his devils.

Having thus recovered his cup, the Brahmin ran home merrily, and he and his wife made a sumptuous feast, such as they had never had before in their lives.

The couple now rejoiced at their good luck, but they wanted many other things besides food. So the wit of the Brahmini suggested to her husband the opening of a confectioner's shop; for, said she, with the money he would get by the sale of his sweets, they could easily supply all their earthly wants.

The Brahmin, who fell in with the suggestion, at once opened a sweetmeat stall, and his sweets, so unlike the ordinary bazaar goods, were very popular, and his fame as a confectioner came to be noised about all over the country.

Now it happened that the King of the country had a beautiful daughter, who was to be wedded to a greater Prince than himself, and he did not know how to entertain the huge party which was sure to accompany the bridegroom to the wedding.

So it befell that the King called a council and placed the matter before his councillors. The Prime Minister, who had heard of the fame of the Brahmin, summoned the latter and ordered him to take charge of the catering for the wedding party. The Brahmin jumped at the offer, seeing visions of gold floating before his eyes.

The wedding day came at last, and the whole party was entertained without difficulty. The Brahmin had produced a variety of viands, which were distributed among the guests, who were seated in separate rows, in order of rank or caste, upon cushions spread upon the ground within a temporary pavilion. They enjoyed the feast thoroughly and soon began to yawn audibly as a sign of satisfaction, or rather of Oriental politeness, for it is thought that, unless one yawns, one's host cannot know whether one has really done full justice to the feast or not.

After the whole party had retired for the night, the Prime Minister said to the King before parting, "May I have, O King! thy word of honour, not to be angry with me?" These words were a sure sign that the Prime Minister was about to advise his sovereign to do something disagreeable :—

"First give thy faith, and plight a prince's word
Of sure protection by thy power and sword,
For I must speak what wisdom would conceal."

The King gave his word of honour, and the Prime Minister urged him to possess himself of the Brahmin's magic cup by force or fraud. "The King," said he, "is the foremost man in his kingdom, and whatever is excellent and best therein belongs by right to him, and the proper place for the Brahmin's food-cup is the royal kitchen."

After that the Brahmin was sent away with a large reward for his excellent catering, but his cup did not go with him.

The Brahmin departed in silence, but none the less determined to teach the King the difference between "mine" and "thine."

The following day the King held a grand durbar, and afterwards gave a farewell entertainment to his guests. Just as he was going round personally with the magic cup in his hand, distributing refreshments to each of them, the Brahmin suddenly arrived with the other cup and handed it to him.

The King, thinking his guests might like a variety in the way of sweets, asked them to try some from the new cup. He at once opened the lid, when lo! instead of sweets, out flew fists, like a swarm of hornets, dealing out hard knocks to everyone present, and there was a general stampede among the guests.

The King, thus humiliated before them, prostrated himself at the feet of the Brahmin, and begged of him to call the fists back into his cup. He did so, and the whole assembly, infuriated at the insult offered them by the King, their host, would have killed him, then and there, but for his profuse apologies for the unfortunate mistake, as he put it, which to some extent pacified them.

For once in a way " virtue " proved something more than " its own reward." The Brahmin was appointed royal chaplain or *guru*, and lived happily ever after.

THE HAWK THE KING-MAKER.

ONCE upon a time there was a pious King in Hindustan, beloved of his subjects, as much for his unstinted liberality to all and sundry as for his just and impartial rule.

He was very fond of holy men, and delighted in their company, and always showered his choicest gifts upon them.

One day a rascal, who pretended that he was a holy man, came to the King and thus said to him: "O Prince! I have lived a recluse in my cell all my life, only now and then stirring out into the great world to visit ancient shrines and places of pilgrimage by the sacred rivers. I feel supremely curious to know what a three days' change in my dull, joyless, ascetic life would feel like. So do thou, O Prince! let me rule over thy kingdom just for three days in thy place."

The King, who never denied aught to any holy men, agreed to this, and with his Queen and his two little sons left his State on a three days' holiday.

The "holy" man now took off his yellow garb, and, putting on his back the gorgeous dress of a Prince, sat on the throne with a golden crown on his head and a jewelled sceptre in his hand, and thus began his three days' reign.

When the stipulated three days' rule was over, the King returned with his family to claim his kingdom, but the so-called holy man, loath to part with the sceptre so soon, thus addressed himself to the King: "O generous Prince! I have tasted of the sweets of power, but my three days' rule has expired too soon. Do thou let me continue to reign for thee over thy kingdom just a little longer."

"A holy man," thought the King to himself, "knows the Scriptures, and this man appears to be one, so he may well be trusted to hold the sceptre for me, for his rule is bound to be just and righteous."

Thus musing, the King consented to part with the sceptre a little longer in favour of the new ruler, and so away he went again with his wife and children, out of his kingdom.

The King and his family travelled from place to place, not knowing where to go, and journeyed on and on until, overcome with hunger and thirst, they came at last to a jungle. Here the King gathered together a few wild fruits and sweet, juicy roots for his wife and children, and with these they somehow appeased their hunger and thirst.

Thus refreshed, the party again resumed their journey, until at nightfall they were obliged to seek shelter at a way-side inn.

Here there happened to be at the time several travellers, and among them a merchant. The latter had secretly trafficked in human flesh, and, as he gazed with wonder upon the charms of the Queen, he at once realized what a nice little fortune there lay in them, could he get hold of her and sell her to someone as a bride.

With this idea uppermost in his mind, he began to set his trap for the unwary Queen. He walked up to the King and introduced himself to him. "I am a merchant," said he, "and have come to do some business in the city which is just a mile from here. I have come on in advance to secure a house suitable for my wife, who is an invalid. She is coming to-morrow evening and may require a little nursing. Shall we go together to the city in the morning and hunt for a quiet, cosy little house such as I want?"

The King, who never lost a chance of doing a good turn to a fellow-man in distress, readily agreed to this, and next morning they set off for the city together, as arranged.

After some aimless wandering up and down the streets, they at last succeeded in finding a nice house in a quiet quarter such as the merchant desired. When everything was apparently settled and done with, they returned to the inn.

The merchant settled his bill with the innkeeper, and, after taking leave of the King, removed, or pretended to remove, to his house.

At dusk the merchant sent a palanquin, a sort of sedan chair borne by two men, with a maid-servant and a note to the King which ran thus: "Dear friend, just as I feared, my wife has arrived quite ill and terribly upset by the journey. May I presume upon our new acquaintance to ask you to be so kind as to send your wife to nurse mine just for the night? I am sending a palanquin and a maid-servant to fetch her here."

The King, who always delighted in good deeds, did not suspect any treachery, so he allowed the Queen to be taken away in the palanquin, with the blinds drawn down, to attend, as he thought, on his friend's wife.

On the morrow the King, accompanied by the two little Princes, went to the house of the merchant, but to his great consternation found the shutters up and no living soul within. Now at length the bitter truth dawned upon him. The merchant had taken away his wife by false pretences. With tears streaming down his cheeks, he searched all over the city for the Queen, but alas! in vain.

Then, in the agony of his despair, leaving her rescue to Providence, he took each of his sons by the hand and went on his way, not caring whithersoever fate might lead them.

Before they had gone very far, however, a stream stopped their progress. The King, unable to get over to the other side burdened with the two Princes, left one on the bank (intending to return and take him across), while he lifted the other on his shoulders and so began to cross the stream. Hardly had he gone half way when a tiger, which had come apparently to drink water, snapped up with a growl the son who had been left behind, and made for the jungle; and as the King all too suddenly turned round to look behind, the boy on his shoulder was jerked into the water and drowned, or carried away by the current.

Thus for the King misfortunes came, not singly, but in battalions. Having lost all his dear and near ones, he journeyed on by himself, beating his breast and rending the air with lamentations like one possessed; and in this condition he came wandering into the territory of another Prince.

By a curious chain of accidents, the latter had just

died, and his ministers, in accordance with the quaint old custom of choosing a successor by lot, took out a hawk and a golden crown, and the hawk was let loose just as the woe-stricken King was entering the city. After circling round and round over the heads of the crowds which had followed close on the heels of the ministers, as if to pick out the fittest one from among them, the hawk finally perched on the head of the newcomer.

At once the ministers gathered round him, put the crown on his head, and carried him triumphantly to the throne. Here he was installed King with full regal honours, and thus once more found himself in his element, and so opened a fresh chapter in his life. He began to rule over his new subjects, as might have been expected, with justice and impartiality, and peace and plenty smiled upon the land as they never had done before. The people were all pleased with his rule, but were distressed to see him always so gloomy and melancholy. The King, they knew, had no Queen, and that, they concluded, was the cause of his sadness. And so, to provide him with a companion, his ministers, without consulting him, inquired far and wide for a suitable bride, at the same time promising a handsome reward to him who found one such as they wanted.

Attracted by the bait of a reward, a man one evening brought a lady endowed with every good quality, and in every respect fit to be a Queen. The ministers, having approved of her as a suitable bride for the King, temporarily left her in a room in the palace, while they themselves prepared to interview the King with the object of inducing him to marry the lady of their choice. Just at this very moment a hunter and a fisherman brought two boys, apparently orphans, and as the King under Hindu law is the guardian of all waifs and strays, they made them over to his ministers. The latter, having asked the boys to wait just outside the room of the Queen-elect, went to the King to advise him to marry the lady they had chosen for him.

The boys, left to themselves in the dim twilight, began to while away their time by narrating the adventures each had gone through, and while they were thus talking, the lady in the room leant forward and listened to their stories, and then, suddenly flinging open the door, fell upon their necks and began to kiss them fervently. She was the kidnapped Queen, and the boys were her own two little Princes, miraculously rescued, one from a tiger's jaws and the other from a watery grave!

While the ministers were suggesting matrimony to the King, a messenger came running to the court and informed him of the strange meeting of the lady with her two lost sons.

The King, accompanied by the whole court, went to witness the scene, when, lo and behold! whom did he see but his own missing Queen, embracing her two dear sons who had been given up for dead:

> "He saw once more his dark-eyed Queen
> Among her children stand;
> They clasped his neck, they kissed his cheeks,
> They held him by the hand."

The wicked merchant was thus balked of his prey, and for his very life ran away as fast as his legs could carry him, while the hunter and the fisherman were sent away with handsome rewards.

Thus did virtue triumph in the end. Nay, more, the pretended holy man having ruled the State with harshness, his subjects rebelled and put him to death, and as the throne can never be without an occupant, the old ministers set out in quest of their former Prince, and, having found him, begged him to return to his kingdom. But as he could not be in two places at one and the same time, he cut the Gordian knot by making each son King of one State with a council of Elders, the Queen and himself retiring into private life in accordance with the immemorial custom amongst the ancients.

THE WAX PRINCE.

ONCE upon a time a certain King was long without an heir to the throne. This made him sad. "Who will," he thought to himself, "carry on my name and line, and, by a chain of descendants, invest me with a sort of immortality on earth? Who will offer oblations to my ancestors and to me after my death?"

One day the King looked more than usually gloomy, and the Queen, for the first time, mustered up sufficient courage to ask him the reason of his sadness.

"O King," said she, "I have often seen you thoughtful. I put it down to the cares and worries of State; but I think that this time I am mistaken. To-day you look unusually gloomy and depressed in spirits. What can be the matter? Do let me know the cause of your mysterious sadness. Perhaps I may be able to relieve your mind of it. At least, sorrow shared is sorrow half relieved, as they say."

"My dear Queen," replied the King with a sigh, "I am myself most unhappy. Why should I make you unhappy too by disclosing the cause of my sorrow?"

The Queen, however, persisted, and at last he spoke as follows:

"O Queen," said he, "I am getting older and older every day. What is troubling me most is the thought of dying without an heir to inherit my throne. Who is to succeed to this vast kingdom? What would become of me and my ancestors? Deprived of filial offerings to our souls, we shall fall headlong into hell."

The Queen took in the situation at a glance. She was herself the cause of all his unhappiness, for she had not yet borne him any heir. Indeed, what wonder, thought she, if he should some day take to wife another princess and so introduce a rival into the palace, since he was so desirous of having an heir? This was not, however, the worst thing she had to fear. Should he have a son by his new wife, the boy would, of course, succeed to the throne, and his mother would be supreme in the palace, while she would be nobody at all. So she called her mother-wit to her assistance, and with a significant smile, which removed all his fears, she said to the King: "Is that, indeed, what is troubling you, O King? Let your mind be set at ease once and for all. I shall soon present you with an heir."

The King leaped up with joy as if he had the moon already in his grasp. Quite beside himself with joy, he said to the Queen, half in earnest, half in jest: "Fie, Queen! How could you have kept this happy news so long to yourself?"

The Queen, putting on a grave face, replied: "O King! I am not altogether to blame for that. I was warned by a dream to keep the news from you, lest it should make you unhappy."

"How could the news really make me unhappy?" exclaimed the King. "Surely, you are joking with me, O Queen!"

"Joking with you? By no means," said the Queen. "Someone in a dream told me I should be the mother of a fair Prince, but that directly you looked upon the child it should die."

Nevertheless, the King felt most happy at the early prospect of an heir. He went straight to the court and proclaimed the happy news there.

There was great rejoicing and merry-making throughout the State. The Queen had already settled in her mind her plan of campaign. She sent for the King and thus said to him: "O King! I do not know when, but I may at any moment present you with an heir. Lest you should, by chance, look on the child, I should like to live quietly by myself in a house away from the palace. You should at once make arrangements for my removal there."

The King thereupon fitted up a house in a quiet neighbourhood for the residence of the Queen.

Time passed on until one day the Queen sent the King news of the " birth " of a Prince.

The King could not, of course, come and see the new-born babe himself, so he sent the Queen a large quantity of gold coins as a gift for the child.

The Queen made full use of the gold, as you may well imagine. With some of it the nurse was won over by her. This very nurse had a few days before been delivered of a boy, and used to bring this child with her into the Queen's room. Whenever the King visited the Queen, the nurse would pinch the ears of the child so as to make it cry with pain. Then she would try to quiet the child by singing lullabies to it. Of course, the foolish King thought it was his own child, and so the fraud remained undetected.

In the fifth year the King sent a tutor to teach the

supposed Prince, and him too the Queen won over with part of the money she still had.

The tutor was in a dilemma. He might have exposed the fraud of the Queen, but he dared not, lest he might thereby incur her displeasure, and possibly her vengeance. For aught he knew, the King might not believe him, and in the first flash of anger might order him to be put to death. On the other hand, thus he argued with himself, if he fell in with the Queen's plans all would be well with him. For one thing, he would not be troubled with any work in the way of teaching, and would get his salary month by month just the same. Then there might be gifts for him into the bargain, and before the fraud could be discovered he would take good care to leave the State, and so be out of the reach of the King.

Thus reasoning with himself, the tutor made up his mind to further the Queen's plans. He used to get other children to supply him with specimens of caligraphy, the best of which he would represent to the King as the work of the Prince, and thus he received valuable gifts for himself.

The King lived on in this fool's paradise until it was time to get the Prince married. The wedding day was fixed. There were great rejoicings throughout the State, and everybody was happy except the Queen, who had a very good reason to be otherwise.

She was in great fear and trembling, for she felt sure that the fraud was now bound to be detected. She did not know what to do to prevent its leaking out. However, once more mother-wit came to her assistance. She made a wax figure of a Prince, so beautiful and lifelike as to make one mistake it for a living person. When everything was ready she put the wax Prince inside the palanquin, and thus said to the King: "I have put the Prince into the palanquin; take care to keep close to it until it arrives at the bride's house. But you must on no account open the door of the palanquin and peep in, or the Prince will fare ill."

The King promised to do as he was bid, and started with a grand procession for the bride's house, where the wedding was to take place. On the way, however, they halted by the bank of a river for a little while, and the palanquin was set down on the bank, with the door slightly ajar to let the breeze in. While it stood there, a snake, which had its abode in the river, crept into the palanquin unobserved, and seeing the wax Prince, got inside the figure and made it alive.

Nothing being noticed, the procession started again, and reached the house of the bride just at the hour fixed for the wedding. There was quite a large number of guests present, and amongst them there were not a few Princes. These, accompanied by the father of the bride, came up to the door of the palanquin to receive the bridegroom.

Directly the door was pushed open, lo and behold! out stepped a young prince, as beautiful as if he were made of wax, and bowed his head gracefully, with a smile to every one present. For the first time, the King looked on the Prince, notwithstanding the Queen's warning; and no sooner had he beheld him than he flung himself on his neck and kissed him.

Soon after, he was seized with remorse lest some misfortune might befall the Prince, but it was too late. The wedding passed off without anything happening to mar it, and the following day the King started back for his kingdom with the Prince and his wife. No sooner did the Queen hear of their coming than she swooned away for very fear. She felt sure her fraud had been discovered, and there was no knowing what the King might do to her in his anger. Coming to the room wherein lay the Queen, the Prince and his bride entered, and finding her apparently asleep, bent down and took the dust off her feet. At this the Queen slowly opened her dazed eyes, and whom should she behold but her own wax Prince standing by her side with the Princess!

She jumped to her feet at once, and received the Prince and the Princess with every outward mark of warmth. The whole thing struck her as if it were a fine piece of stage acting. She thought her wax Prince must have been clothed with flesh and blood and then made alive by some magician or other.

This was not, however, the time to show her surprise. She blessed the pair and welcomed the Princess to the palace. Nevertheless, however much she may have lavished her affections upon the wax Prince, she used to fear him and dared not look him in the face.

One day the Princess said to the Queen: "O Queen! I, who have just been introduced into the family, long to hear something of its history."

This proved a capital opportunity for the Queen to satisfy her own curiosity as to how her wax Prince had turned into flesh and blood, and so she replied: "O Princess! I am hardly more versed in that than yourself, and do not know the history of this family half as well as your husband does. I am sure he will tell you if you ask him."

One evening, the Prince and Princess were walking together along the bank of the river near the place where the palanquin containing the wax Prince had rested, and the Princess asked her husband of what race he was. "Princess! do not be too curious," the wax Prince warned her. "Ask me anything else you like but that, and I will tell you."

This rather whetted her feminine curiosity, so she at once begged and coaxed him to tell her who he was.

The wax Prince went down into the water and warned her once more: "Princess!" said he, "do not try to know what is not good for you. Knowledge is a poor exchange for happiness."

As he said this, his feet at once changed into the tail of a snake, but the Princess could not see it under the water in the dark, and still insisted upon his answering her question. "Princess!" said the Prince, "then you still want to know who I am?" She said, "Yes." And lo! the tail extended right up to his waist. Still the Princess persisted, and the Prince, going down into still deeper water, said, "Princess, do you still want to know who I am?" The Princess took it all to be a joke, so she said, "Yes." And this time the tail extended right up to the Prince's shoulder. For the last time the wax Prince warned the Princess, saying, "Princess, do you still want to know who I am?"

"You have repeated the same question thrice over," said the Princess. "If you love me, tell me of what race you are!"

The wax Prince at once became a huge snake which reared its gigantic hood, and, with a terrific hiss, plunged down into the water and disappeared.

The Princess, seeing her husband change into a snake, fell straightway into a swoon, and, when she came to herself, found she had been brought to a hut by a kind-hearted old woman who had gone down to the river to fetch water. The whole strange tragedy seemed to the Princess to be an evil dream, and, not daring to return to her father-in-law's house without the Prince, she decided to stay on with the old woman.

When the Prince and the Princess failed to return to the palace, the King became very anxious about them, and suspected with reason (for had he not looked on the Prince, notwithstanding the Queen's warning ?) that some misfortune must have happened to them.

However, a long search was made for the missing couple, far and near, but of neither the Prince nor the Princess could any trace be found. The worst fears of the King were now realized. " I told you so," said the Queen to the King, " yet despite my warning you looked on the Prince. Something has undoubtedly happened to him and his wife." There was now weeping, as before there had been rejoicing throughout the State.

Time went by. A curious incident, however, was noticed at the house of the old woman. Every afternoon a big snake used to come from the direction of the river and sit coiled up at the feet of the Princess, and even showed a disposition to play with her ; and, as he did her absolutely no harm, she grew fond of him, and would feed him on milk and cream with her own hand.

The news of this extraordinary incident, as one might have expected, spread far and wide, and at last reached the ears of the King, who, one afternoon, attracted by curiosity, went to the old woman's house secretly, and hid himself behind the trunk of a tree.

The Princess had just fallen ill and was asleep in her room, with the old woman sitting by her. Before he had been long there, the snake came crawling to the house from the direction of the river, and, not finding the Princess in her accustomed seat, began to circle round the room in an agitated manner. Hurriedly looking round to make sure that no one was near, the snake threw off his slough, and lo and behold! out stepped the wax Prince and walked straight into the Princess's room. The King, who had been watching all this from behind the tree, then seized the slough and burnt it up.

After that, he rushed to the room of the Princess, and before the wax Prince could get away he found himself confronted with the King, who caught him in his arms with cries of joy. "Wax Prince" (for that was the name he went by), "where have you been so long?" cried out the King. At the mention of the name "wax Prince," the Princess sat up in her bed with a start, when whom did she see but the King holding the wax Prince in his embrace! Joyfully did the King return to the palace with his long-lost son and daughter-in-law. The old woman, too, accompanied them, and was well cared for all the rest of her life.

THE GOLDEN PARROT.

Once upon a time there was a King who had seven sons. He was very fond of birds, and he had a large collection of some of the rarest species in the world. He used to amuse himself by listening to their songs and gazing at their plumage.

One day, while listening to the songs of his birds, he fell asleep and dreamt a curious dream. A ghostly form appeared before him and said: "O Prince! you have certainly some of the finest singing birds in the world, but none of them can compare with the Golden Parrot in the possession of the Queen of the Peris (Fairies), who lives on a floating island. If you could possess yourself of this parrot you would want no other bird."

Next morning, the King got up from his bed early, and, calling his seven sons together, said to them: "My dear sons, you know how fond I am of birds. I have collected many rare kinds from various lands, but none of these rival the beauty of the Golden Parrot to be found on a certain floating island guarded by Peris. Should any of you secure this bird for me, I would give him half my kingdom as a reward, even during my lifetime. I would make absolutely no distinction between the eldest and the youngest in this respect."

On hearing this, six of his sons became very much excited, and, fastening their swords to their belts, offered to set off at once in quest of the Golden Parrot. Before starting, however, they said to the youngest brother: "You see we are going out to fetch the Golden Parrot. We may or may not succeed in our adventure; there may be many trials and difficulties in our way which cannot yet be foreseen. So, to ascertain whether we are in danger or not, you must keep a bowl of milk on the roof with an arrow stuck in the middle, bolt upright. Should any danger overtake us, the milk is sure to turn reddish in colour. If the arrow tumbles down, that will mean our approaching doom. As soon as you find the milk turning red, come to our rescue if you can."

With these words, the brothers set out with a light heart in quest of the Golden Parrot. On they journeyed merrily until dusk, when they sought shelter at an inn for the night.

Inns are sometimes frequented by robbers disguised as travellers. It so happened that some clever thieves followed close upon the heels of these Princes, and they all entered the inn close together. The innkeeper had no idea whether the robbers formed a separate band of travellers, or were members of the Princes' party. In the end, however, he put them up together.

When the Princes had fallen asleep, the robbers ransacked their rooms and seized everything they could lay their hands upon, and then, mounting their horses, rode quietly away.

The next morning the Princes found that they had been robbed overnight. They went and complained to the innkeeper of the robbery, but the latter at once put them down as rogues and cheats.

"Well," said the innkeeper to the Princes, "where are your friends? You have sent all your things away securely by them in advance, and now you want to cheat me of my dues. You must either pay me what is owing, or else submit to be my slaves until you have earned sufficient to clear off your debt."

As there was no other alternative, they had to submit to the innkeeper's terms, and so began a life of slavery in his service.

In the meantime the youngest Prince noticed the milk in the bowl turning reddish, so, thinking that his brothers were in distress, he set out in search of them, hoping at the same time to bring back the Golden Parrot for the King.

He journeyed from place to place until he came upon an old hermit in a state of profound meditation and unconscious of his surroundings; a hollow in an ant-heap formed his cell, while the tendrils of many a creeper crept in and out through his matted hair, and the hermit himself looked like a piece of statuary.

The Prince tore away the creepers, cleaned up his cell, and waited upon him with joined palms.

One day the old ascetic opened his dazed eyes and looked on the Prince in attendance upon him. He was pleased with his devotion, and requested him to ask for whatever boon he pleased as a reward.

The Prince said, "I want the Golden Parrot which has been dreamt of by my father."

"Ask for anything," the hermit replied, "but the Golden Parrot."

But the Prince persisted: "I ask for no other boon; either the Golden Parrot or nothing."

Thereupon the old man said to the Prince: "Thou hast set thy heart upon a mad task. Thou knowest not what dangers lie in thy way. Thou mayest lose thy life for thy pains."

Still the Prince persisted: "Cost what it may, I am determined to risk everything for it."

"O silly youth," the ascetic thus began, "since thou hast set thy heart upon the Golden Parrot, lend me thine ear. Hard by this hermitage is a lake frequented by Peris for their morning bath. Before going down into the water they are wont to take off their wings and leave them on the bank. Get hold of a pair of these if thou canst, and with them fly after the Peris, but out of range of their sight. At noon the Peris have their afternoon sleep, and then is thy chance. Go into the quarters of the Queen of the Peris, seize the bird, and fly back with it to me as fast as thou art able. Remember thou carriest thy life in thy hand."

The Prince thanked the hermit, and, according to his instructions, betook himself to the spot where the Peris were in the habit of depositing their wings, and hid himself in a tree near by.

Shortly afterwards a band of them came flying through the air, took off their wings, and, flinging them down beneath the tree, plunged into the water.

While the Peris were engaged in bathing and swimming, the Prince came down from the tree stealthily, and, putting on a pair of wings, lay in hiding in the neighbourhood of the lake.

One by one the Peris came out of the water, and, putting on their wings, flew away towards their island home, followed by the Prince at a safe distance.

In the meantime the Peri whose wings were stolen could not, of course, find them when she came out of the water, and looked for them everywhere.

In the course of her search she came to the hermitage, and, seeing the ascetic, accused him of stealing her wings.

The ascetic feigned to be in a great rage and said to the Peri: "Darest thou call me a thief? Dost thou not know I am a great saint and can consume thee with the fire of my wrath?"

The Peri then fell at his feet and begged his pardon, and requested him to help her to find her wings.

Of course the hermit knew who had taken away her wings, and that there would be no use for them after the Golden Parrot had been seized. So, to occupy her time until the Prince came back, he took her round the lake and pretended to search for them.

The day wore on till noon, and the ascetic was expecting the Prince back every moment. He turned to the Peri and said: "Do you rest awhile by this lake. I forgot I expected a guest at noon, so let me get back to the hermitage and fetch him; we shall both join you in search again, presently."

Of course the guest was no other than the Prince, who, following the instructions of the ascetic, had succeeded in bringing away the Golden Parrot and returned to the hermitage soon after.

"Well done, my boy!" said the hermit to the Prince, as he looked at the Golden Bird. "Now, come after me to the lake: but take care to hide the wings you have in a hole somewhere."

The Prince did as he was bid, and then came on to where the ascetic and the Peri had been searching for the wings. At last, guided by the Prince, the Peri saw something of a rosy hue inside a hole. She peeped in and, with cries of joy, exclaimed: "Here are my wings! Here are my wings!" The Prince then crept into the hole and brought them out for her.

The Peri was now convinced that her suspicions against the ascetic were unfounded. She thought the wings must have been seized and carried away into the hole by a jackal or some other animal, while she was sporting in the water.

Pleased with the Prince, she gave him a golden flute as a reward, saying, "If you ever get into any trouble, you need only blow the flute at midnight,—remember, only at midnight and no other hour!—and I will come to your succour."

The Peri then put on her wings and flew away gaily. Soon afterwards, the Prince took his leave of the ascetic, and, taking the Golden Parrot with him, set out in search of his brothers.

In the course of his wanderings, he happened to halt at the inn where his brothers were working as the slaves of the innkeeper. He walked up to the latter and offered to redeem his brothers by paying him their dues. To this the innkeeper agreed, and, after the Prince had paid what was owing and had left the inn, his brothers were released with the brands of the innkeeper on them. They knew nothing, of course, of this change of masters. They thought they had worked out their debts and had been restored to liberty.

The six brothers then set off for their native country, but, before they had gone far, they met their youngest brother with the Golden Parrot. They were filled with envy to find him successful where they had failed. They knew that, if he was allowed to go home alive with the Golden Parrot, he was sure to get half the kingdom as a reward. So they decided to rob him of the bird and get him out of their way, for a dead man tells no tales, and they, by presenting the Parrot to their father, would get half the kingdom between them.

After this wicked decision, they happened to rest by a well, where one of them, pretending to be thirsty, was about to draw water, when the youngest brother volunteered to do it for him. As he bent down to draw the water, the wicked brothers pushed him in, and taking possession of the Parrot, went on their way.

Thus it was that the young Prince found himself at the bottom of the well, but, as it still wanted some hours to midnight, he could not blow the flute for assistance. Punctually as the hour of midnight arrived, he blew the golden flute he had on his person, when lo and behold! his friend, the Peri, came flying through the air. She drew the Prince out of the well, and then, lifting him upon her wings, carried him straight off to his father's kingdom, and put him down just in front of the King and Queen, as they were walking together in their park.

The King, surprised at this strange sight, received him with joy, feeling sure he had succeeded in his search for the Golden Parrot. The Prince assured his father his brothers were bringing it with them.

Shortly afterwards, the six elder sons arrived with the Golden Parrot, and, presenting it to the King, asked him to share the kingdom with them, according to his promise. Of course, they took it for granted that their youngest brother was dead and gone, so what was their astonishment to find him safe and sound at home! They thought at first it was his ghost, but turned pale with fear as soon as they realised he was really flesh and blood.

The young Prince then told the King how he had found his brothers working as the slaves of an innkeeper, how they had been branded with red-hot irons, how he had redeemed them, how they had behaved wickedly to him by throwing him down a well and robbing him of the Parrot, and all the rest of his adventures.

The King then ordered his six sons to disrobe themselves, and sure enough, the branding was distinctly visible on their bodies, as the youngest brother had said.

The King turned his six wicked sons out of his kingdom, and he and his youngest son reigned over their subjects happily.

THE TABLES TURNED.

ONCE upon a time there were two neighbours, but, contrary to what neighbours ought to do, they bore very little love towards each other. One was a fool, but rich beyond the dreams of avarice, and the other was a Sage who lived by his wits. Whenever they met, they were sure to quarrel and wrangle like school children. The fool would taunt the Sage for being poor in spite of his wisdom, and the latter would taunt him in return with ten-fold interest. So they lived on, and so they would have gone on living to the end of the chapter, but for a strange event.

Once they met, and, as usual, fell to quarrelling, and this time their quarrel seems to have reached its climax. "Thou pratest words of wisdom, to be sure," said the fool to the Sage, "but, for all that, thou art as poor as a church-mouse."

"And thou wearest a King's ransom on thy back," retorted the sage, "but carriest an ass's head on thy shoulders, for all that. Thou braggest so of thy wealth, but all thy gold is no match for my wits."

At this the fool became very angry, and said: "Prove that if thou canst, and, should thy wits succeed where my gold fails, I will willingly go shares with thee in all my wealth. Let us put the matter to the test at once."

"Agreed," said the Sage, and away went both to the King of the land and prayed him to act as judge and decide the quarrel between them. The King looked at them with a mischievous twinkle in his eye, then sat down and wrote a short note, and, after sealing it, threw it towards them with a chuckle, saying: "Take this to my brother King over the frontier, and he will decide your quarrel for me. Neither of you will ever have occasion to quarrel any more, I am sure."

And so with light hearts they crossed the frontier together and presented the note to the King for whom it was intended. The latter broke open the seal and read out its contents—"Pray put the bearers of this to death at once."

The fool, the Sage, and the King stared at each other in blank amazement. The two neighbours now found themselves caught in a trap and were at their wits' end to decide what to do to save their necks from the gallows. Verily, for them it proved a case of falling out of the frying-pan into the fire.

The Sage now took his rich neighbour aside and told him to save his own life by his gold if he could, without minding about himself; and the latter tried to bribe everybody from the King to the executioner with gold, if they would only let him escape death, but all in vain. The King turned a deaf ear to all his prayers and entreaties for mercy, and none of his officers dared to disobey him.

Now the fool turned to the Sage and said to him, in a tone tremulous with fear: "Well, for once my gold has failed. Now it is thy turn to try and save our lives by thy wits if thou canst, and, if thou succeedest, half of my wealth will be thine, according to our compact."

The King then ordered them to be taken away at once to the place of execution; but, when they were being removed from his presence, the Sage broke out into a loud burst of mock laughter, and the King, seeing him laugh while he should be weeping, asked him the reason of his strange behaviour, and out came this story: "O King!" said the Sage, "thou art anxious to know the reason of my laughter, and well mayest thou be anxious to know it for thine own sake. A hoary-headed astrologer," went on the Sage, setting his wits to work, "once came to the court of our King and predicted, with a solemn wag of his beard, all sorts of misfortunes for his kingdom, so long as we two wretches, as he was pleased to call us, were permitted to live in his State. 'They are most unlucky fellows,' said the astrologer, 'but do not thou kill them for that, or else their ill-luck will be transferred to thee and thy kingdom. Get them put to death by some other Prince, for that will be killing two birds with one stone. In the first place, thou wilt thus be rid of them, and, directly they are slain, their ill-luck will be transferred to their slayer, and his kingdom will fall an easy prey to thine arms.' Of course, nothing was thought of it at the time, and we took it for a joke. Now we are undeceived."

This story had its expected effect, and all the assembled courtiers, with one voice, advised the King to let the men go. There must be some truth in what this man said, they declared, for they might just as well have been executed in their own country, instead of being sent so far away over the frontier without any reason being given.

Now the King became very angry, and sent the men back to their country with a sealed message for their King, which he delivered into their hands. They prostrated themselves to the ground and went back home as fast as their legs could carry them.

As soon as they reached their own country, they presented themselves before their King, and the Sage, with an ill-concealed chuckle, put the sealed letter into his hands. The King was surprised to see the wretches back alive, and, breaking open the seal, he read the message, and as he read it he turned deadly pale. The message was as short as the one he had sent to the frontier King, and read thus: "This letter is sent to inform you that I declare war against you."

The King, surprised and frightened beyond all measure, asked the Sage the meaning of it all, and the latter stepped forward and repeated the story he had told the frontier King, with such good results for himself and his friend.

The King now remembered the chuckle of the Sage, and said to him and his friend, the fool: "You must not shout before you are out of the wood. You are congratulating yourselves on having escaped death, but you cannot escape it now at my hands." And, so saying, he ordered them to be put to death at once. The fool sought to save his life with his gold and, having failed once more, resigned himself to his fate. When they were being removed from the presence of their King, the Sage again broke out into a burst of mock laughter, as he had done before the foreign Prince. The King, surprised at his conduct, enquired the reason of it, and the Sage thus replied to him: "O King! I am glad thou hast asked the reason of my laughter, for thy kingdom depends on our lives. We two are more than a match for any army the foreign King may send, yet thou art, so to speak, lopping off the very branch on which thou art seated. That it was that provoked my laughter."

Thereupon the King said: "Very well, prove what you say by your deeds. If you can drive back the invading army, I will spare your lives, but if you fail to carry out your boast, remember I will order you to be thrown among a pack of dogs, to be torn to pieces limb from limb as a punishment for all your wicked lies."

Neither the Sage nor the fool had ever ridden a horse or handled a weapon in their lives, so they had to be strapped on to their horses that they might not fall, and swords were hung to their belts.

Directly they saw the foreign King coming with an army, they rode up to him, and, interposing themselves between him and his army, said to him: "O Prince! before thou advancest one step further, thou must either fight us or return to thy kingdom."

The Prince and his army became very much frightened lest some misfortune might come to them since they had looked on the faces of the two most unlucky men in the world. "If I fight and kill these two wretches," thought the Prince to himself, "I shall lose my kingdom, according to the prediction of the soothsayer; and as they will not budge an inch and are so eager to die at our hands, there must be some reason for it; so it will be safer to leave the wretches and their country alone." Thus musing, the King returned with his army over the frontier, and the Sage and the fool returned to the King with the glad news.

The King was pleased with their bravery, and, as a reward for their services, not only spared their lives, but gave them the highest ranks and honours in his patronage.

Now, according to the compact, the fool exchanged half his gold for the Sage's begging-bowl, but the latter returned the wealth he had thus won by his wits with the question: "What dost thou say now? Have not my wits been more than a match for all thy gold?"

"Yes," replied the fool, and from that time forward the two lived together on the best of terms.

THE PRINCESS WITH THE BORROWED LIFE.

Once upon a time there was a King who had an only son, but for some reason or other the latter had incurred his father's displeasure and, with his wife, had been banished from the kingdom.

The unfortunate couple took shelter in a forest, which was then nobody's property, and the Princess, wearied out with her long tramp, fell into a deep slumber, while her husband lay awake, keeping watch lest any harm should come to her; but, as ill-luck would have it, a deadly snake, which had its hole close by, crept out stealthily and bit the Princess.

The Prince, seeing her dead, set up a loud lamentation, which attracted to the spot a forest-hermit.

"Why dost thou weep, my son?" said the latter to the Prince, as he looked upon the Princess. "Thy wife was never destined to live long."

"Canst thou not, holy father," said the Prince, almost beside himself with grief, "bring her to life again?"

"Yes," replied the hermit, "if thou wilt part with twenty out of the allotted years of thy life to thy wife."

This the Prince speedily promised, and the hermit then asked him to join the palms of the dead Princess's hands together so as to form a cup ; which done, he put into them a little water out of his gourd and then asked him to say to his wife—" Wake up, my wife ! I part with twenty out of the allotted years of my life unto thee."

No sooner was this said than she sat up with a start, as if nothing had happened to her beyond an evil dream, and that very moment the hermit disappeared into the forest like an apparition.

After this the royal couple did not consider it safe to dwell in the forest any longer, so they took to tramping once more, until after many adventures they found a home in a family of amateur dancers and singers.

The Princess was extremely fond of these arts and soon acquired remarkable proficiency as a dancer. Then, in order to judge by the test of public applause whether she had, in fact, attained such proficiency, she one day put on a disguise and slipped out with her friend, to give public exhibitions of her newly-acquired art.

The Prince, her husband, made a search for her, but, unable to discover her whereabouts, he reconciled himself to his fate at last, and took service with a nobleman, a high dignitary of the country.

Time passed on. The kingdom was astir with grand preparations for a festival, and the King had invited every nobleman in the kingdom to the palace to witness a performance by a famous dancer.

The Prince accompanied his master to the palace to witness the dance—and what a dance ! The spectators were charmed no less with the dancing and singing than with the beauty of the performer, and applause greeted her at every turn, and gifts of great value poured in upon her. Among these gifts was a ring from the Prince, and, as she took it in her hand and looked at it, the dancer saw that it was her own ring with her name engraved on it, which she had exchanged for her husband's at her wedding; but she did not notice who among the crowd had given it to her.

After the dance was over, the spectators gathered round her, complimenting her in Oriental hyperbole on her splendid performance, and showering gifts upon her; for their hearts were captivated by her dazzling beauty.

The King himself came round and lavished his praise upon her, and asked her what she wished him to do for her.

The lady handed him the ring and said: "Your Highness! this ring belongs to me. Someone among the crowd presented it to me. He must be the thief. I beg your Highness to find out who it is and punish him."

As soon as the Prince heard the accusation made against him—for it was he who had given her the ring—he stepped forward, rubbed his eyes well, and discovered that the lady who had captivated the hearts of all the spectators, as well as his own, by her beauty, and who had won their applause by her exquisite dancing, was none other than his missing spouse, the Princess herself.

The Prince turned round and said to the King: "I gave this ring to this lady. She is my wife; but she left me some time ago and has since taken to the life of a dancing girl. I did not recognize her at the time I gave her the ring. If she wants further proof, I say that she would have died of snake-bite, had I not revived her at the expense of a part of my life; and yet, for all that, she calls me a thief in public."

The Princess, of course, knew nothing of all this, and took the Prince for an impostor. She burst out into sarcastic laughter at what she imagined was but an idle tale, and challenged him to prove it all to her.

The Prince then asked her to join her palms together in the shape of a cup, and, as soon as that was done, he put a little water into them and said: "I have lent thee twenty of the best years of my life. I take them back." No sooner was this said than the Princess staggered and dropped down dead on the spot!

The spectators were horrified at the sight, and would have beaten the Prince to death, then and there; but the King interfered, and, having heard the real truth from his lips, offered him his daughter in marriage, and the couple lived together long and happily.

THE HERMIT CAT.

Once upon a time a tom cat, grown too old and infirm to catch his prey, stationed himself before the door of a temple, and fed on the crumbs of the offerings made to the idol by its votaries. Sometimes he used to sally out, holding up a rosary in one fore-paw, carrying a begging-bowl in the other, and limping along on his hind legs, in the hope of catching his prey by pious fraud instead of force, after the fashion of robber-mendicants.

On one of these sallies, the cat met with a mouse, and the latter, surprised to see a cat turned hermit, was bold enough to ask him whither he was bound.

"I have been abroad on a pilgrimage," said the cat. "I have just returned, and am now bound for my temple."

The mouse, prostrating himself before the cat, at a sufficiently safe distance, for "what is bred in the bone will come out in the flesh," begged to be allowed to accompany him. Of course, the request was granted, the mouse following the hermit at a respectful distance.

The cat could not, even if he would, catch the mouse on open ground, lacking the energy to pursue his prey; but, once inside the temple, he could, said he to himself, pen him in and capture him with ease.

A little further on, a pigeon with a tuft of feathers on his head joined the party.

Arrived at the temple, the cat made his companions walk in, and himself stood at the door, telling the rosary as if he were engaged in prayer, so as to disarm the suspicions of his intended victims.

In the meantime the mouse, suspecting foul play, made a sufficiently long hole for himself in the floor of the temple, while the pigeon perched himself on the canopy over the idol, beyond the cat's reach.

After a time, hungry as he was, the cat lost patience, and cast about for an excuse before attacking his intended victims.

In a tone of haughtiness he demanded of the pigeon why he wore a tuft of feathers on his head.

"The tuft of feathers," said the bird with much humility, "is worn as a badge of caste."

The cat next turned to the mouse and demanded, in a still more haughty tone, why he wore a beard and whiskers.

"My beard and whiskers, thy holiness," replied the mouse, "are as much symbols of my religion as thy rosary and begging-bowl are of thine."

The cat, who now saw he had been found out, at once sprang upon the mouse, but, before his palsied paws could touch him, the little animal had slipped into the newly-made hole, while, as for the pigeon, it flew away to a place of safety.

Balked of his prey, the cat sulkily left the temple, and went and sat under a tree by a mouse-hole, with three paws up, sustaining his whole weight upon the fourth. The mice issued out of the hole, and, seeing the cat standing on one paw, enquired why he was practising austerities in front of their hole, of all places on earth. The cat winked at them and said: "I am a cat turned hermit. I am standing on one paw out of consideration for mother Earth, because, if I stood on all four, she would be burdened with a greater weight."

The mice took him to be a very religious cat, and ceased to have any fear of him, and so, as they filed past, they prostrated themselves before him.

The wily cat used to snap up the last of the mice as they went past him, and, after they were gone out of sight, would devour him.

In this way his religious garb stood him in good stead, but, on the other hand, the mice kept missing some one or other of their numerous family every day. One missed her husband, another his wife, a third his sister, and so on, and there was much weeping and lamentation among the survivors, and their suspicions naturally fell upon the cat-hermit, the hereditary enemy of their tribe.

They accordingly determined to keep watch over the doings of the cat-hermit, and, as they filed out of the hole, the head of the party kept looking behind until the last mouse had left, and lo! as the latter came out, he was seized! The party then turned back, and the cat instantly let go his prey and resumed his former attitude. The mice filed back into the hole, and, acting on the principle of "union is strength," caught hold of the cat's tail and dragged him, by sheer force of numbers, into the hole, and made a feast off him, which lasted for many and many a day.

THE CROP OF FRIED MAIZE.

ONCE upon a time a half-witted farmer took it into his head to grow a crop of fried maize, or Indian corn. " How nice it would be," said he to himself, " to grow fried maize on my field. I could then eat the maize without any trouble, and there would be no need of fire or fuel to cook it."

He then proceeded to put his brilliant idea into execution. First he fried a quantity of maize grains, then he ploughed up a field and sowed them. As might have been expected, nothing came up, with the exception of one solitary seed which had escaped the frying-pan.

At midnight the celestial elephant of Indra, the Giant-Killer and King of the Gods, used to come down from heaven to feed and disport himself in the field and its neighbourhood, and he used to leave behind him large circular foot-marks, resembling grind-stones. The crazy farmer thought that all his neighbours' grind-stones came out at night on to his field and ate up all the maize-grains. So one night he kept watch, and lo ! towards midnight, down came a huge elephant from the clouds upon his land, and when, after some time, it was about to reascend to heaven, the farmer just caught hold of his tail and was thus carried upwards.

Indra, surrounded by all his celestial *Apsaras* and *Gandharvas* (elves and fairies), then happened to be holding a carnival, and the farmer slipped in amongst them. He had a huge turban on his head, folded round and round, as if it were a coiled-up serpent, and the turban made him the "observed of all observers" among the gods and goddesses.

Indra, surprised to see a mortal in heaven, asked who had brought him there. The farmer told him how he had been dragged up to heaven, clinging to the tail of the elephant. Indra listened to all he had to say, and then, taking a fancy to his turban, gave him a handful of shining, celestial gold coins in exchange for it. After this the farmer came down to earth again in the same way as he had ascended, and spread out the shining gold coins before the admiring gaze of his neighbours.

Desiring to get rich in a night, in a similar manner, his friends entreated him to introduce them to Indra. He agreed, and, following his instructions, they all assembled before midnight wearing huge turbans on their heads, hoping to be transported to heaven. At midnight, as was his wont, the celestial elephant came down to his favourite field, and, after having fed and disported himself, began to ascend to heaven. The crazy farmer caught hold of his tail just in the nick of time, whilst his neighbours hung on to him one behind the other, and thus began to make the ascent.

While high up in the air, one of the neighbours, filled with dreams of gold, asked the short-witted farmer what was the length of the turban which he had sold for so much money to Indra. The farmer immediately let go his hold of the elephant's tail in order to show with his hands how long his turban was, when down they all fell with the farmer on top of them, and all but he were killed outright.

Thus came to an end the farmer's dreams of unlimited wealth, and from that time onward he was a sadder and a wiser man.

THE MONKEY BRIDEGROOM.

ONCE upon a time a monkey, while up a tree pilfering fruit, had his tail pricked by a thorn. He hastily jumped down from the tree, with some fruit, and ran straight to the surgeon, a barber.

"Sir Barber," said the monkey, addressing him politely, "wilt thou be pleased to draw the thorn out of my tail and take this fruit in reward for thy pains?"

The barber eyed the monkey with some misgiving, thinking he had come to make fun of him. He took hold of his tail, however, and searched for the thorn for a long, long while, but could not find it; and so, at last, losing all patience, he cut the tail right off at the root with his razor, and, holding it up to the monkey, said to him, laughing, "What a big thorn! Isn't it?"

The monkey, not to be outwitted, snatched away the barber's razor in compensation for his tail, and bolted.

On the way, he came upon an old man plucking grass with his hand and putting it on a blanket. The monkey generously offered him the razor, and the old man, who was loud in his thanks, at once began to cut the grass with it.

Grinning from ear to ear, the monkey watched him at his work, and soon the razor became blunted.

"What!" said the monkey, springing to his feet, "thou hast blunted my razor! I must have something in return for it." And away he ran with the old man's blanket.

Throwing it round him, he proceeded on his way till he met a man carrying some sugar in a small sack, from which some was running out; and the monkey at once offered his blanket to him. The man thanked his kind-hearted friend, and, pouring the sugar into the blanket, folded it up in the shape of a bag, and, tying it with a knot at the top, flung the bundle over his shoulder and went on his way, with the monkey following close at his heels; but still the sugar kept leaking out.

"Thou hast torn my valuable blanket," said the monkey. "Thou must compensate me for it." And away he ran with the sugar wrapped up in the blanket.

A little further on, he saw an old woman boiling milk, with her little grand-child in her lap. He walked up to her, and, placing the sugar before her, said, "Madam, wilt thou be pleased to make some sweets for me?"

The woman thanked him and made some delicious sweets out of the sugar and milk. She placed these on a dish, giving one to her grand-child to quiet its crying.

The monkey immediately cried out: "What right hadst thou, madam, to give any of my sweets away without my leave? For that thou shalt have none." And, saying that, he carried the dish of sweets away to make up for the sugar he had lost.

Next he met two men carrying a little girl in a palanquin borne on their shoulders. They sat down under a shady tree by a well, and, feeling thirsty, began to drink water, when the monkey, coming up from behind, offered the sweets to them. They were very much pleased with him for his timely offer, and did justice to the sweets, and, as they got up to go, they handed back the empty dish to the monkey.

"What, thou art coolly handing me an empty dish, and no payment for my sweets! I must have the girl for my bride." And with that he seized the girl, and bolted.

"Thou must wed me and be my bride," said the monkey to the girl, as he carried her away.

"How can I marry thee, a mere monkey?" replied the girl, frightened; but the monkey assured her he was only a mannikin and not a monkey, for all monkeys have tails, but he had none.

"Well," said the girl, somewhat recovered from her surprise, "who is to wed us?" The monkey then went up to a Brahmin who was reading his scriptures, and begged him to marry them.

In the meantime the parents of the girl were on the track of the runaways, and came upon them while they were still in the company of the Brahmin. They at once took the girl away home, but the monkey in his bridal robes followed them behind, crying: "O give me back my bride! O give me back my bride! She is mine by fair exchange."

As they went into the house, they slammed the door upon the monkey, keeping him out, but the latter persistently kept knocking at the door, and saying: "O give me back my bride! O give me back my bride! She is mine by fair exchange. I exchanged my tail for a razor, my razor for a blanket, my blanket for sugar, my sugar for sweetmeats, and my sweetmeats for a bride. O give me back my bride! O give me back my bride!"

"What a silly son-in-law thou art!" cried out the girl's mother to the monkey, from behind the closed door. "O what a noise thou dost make for nothing! Thou wouldst not give us time to prepare a fitting reception for thee. Have the patience, my dear son-in-law, to wait just a little longer till I call for thee." At this the monkey was mollified and waited patiently.

In the meantime the girl's mother had set up a seat stuck all over with pins, points up, with a piece of embroidered cloth over it, and then, coming to the door and leading the monkey by the hand to the seat, prayed him to be seated.

The monkey-bridegroom, feeling greatly pleased with the right royal reception accorded him, flung himself down on the spiked seat with a heavy thud Instantly springing up and crying out with pain, he exclaimed: "Dear me! mother-in-law, what stinging vermin thou hast got in thy house!" and bolted out of the room, howling with pain, and vowing never, never again to play the bridegroom.

THE WOODEN MAID.

ONCE upon a time a beautiful girl, who had been married, according to custom, when a child, had grown up, and as yet her husband had not come to claim her. Her parents, while awake in bed, one stifling mid-summer night, began to speak about this, and expressed to each other their wonder at his not having come to take her to his home.

A thief, who happened to be in hiding in the room, waiting for a chance to rob them, overheard the conversation, and, transported with joy at the prospect of a bigger haul than he had expected, left them in peace for the night.

On the morrow, however, he and some accomplices came to the girl's father with a palanquin, and, giving themselves out to be messengers from her husband, begged him to let them take her away.

The father, who had long expected his daughter to be sent for, took the robbers at their word, and sent her off, loaded with jewellery, to her husband as he thought,

The robbers were overjoyed with their booty, and bore her on their shoulders in the palanquin, with the blinds drawn down.

On the way, fatigued and hungry, they put the palanquin down in an empty house a little way off the main road, and, leaving it in charge of a small street urchin, went off to the nearest shop for refreshments and a smoke.

Meanwhile, the girl's suspicions having been roused, she stepped out of the palanquin, called the boy to her side, and asked him to put his tongue out. No sooner had he done this than the girl cut it out with a sharp knife, which she had concealed on her person, and then, putting a few heavy stones into the palanquin in her place, just to ward off the robbers' suspicions, she ran off and climbed up into a mango-tree.

Shortly afterwards the robbers returned refreshed, and, taking the palanquin up on their shoulders again, went on their way; but the boy ran after them, crying, "Mama, mama." He meant by this to imply that the girl was hiding up in the mango-tree, but as he had lost his tongue he could only say "Mama."

"Go home to thy mama, thou suckling babe," said one of the robbers, thrusting him aside and throwing a copper to him. After the robbers were gone, the girl came down from the mango-tree, and, taking all her jewellery off her person and hiding it in the folds of her flowing robe, went straight to a carpenter and ordered him to make a disguise of bark for her to fit her body closely, and thus make her appear as if she were a wooden maid.

The carpenter executed the order to her satisfaction, and was rewarded with part of her jewellery for his labour.

Clad in this disguise, she hastened to the house of her husband and took service with him. Of course her identity could not be discovered because of her wooden covering.

"Who art thou, and what is thy name?" asked the husband.

"Thou seest," replied the maiden, "that I am a wooden maid, and by that name thou must call me, as I have no name of my own."

"What canst thou do, my pretty wooden maid?" asked the husband again.

"I am sure I do not know," replied the maid, "but I think I could tend cattle as well as any cowherd."

"Very well," said the husband, "thou canst tend my cattle, then."

So it came about that she used to take the cattle to the pastures every day, and at noon she would take off her disguise and bathe in the river. She loved living among the oxen, and at all times of the day one might hear her singing in the fields.

The gentle tones of the maiden, however, reminded her employer of his long-neglected wife, and he at once despatched messengers to fetch her. Arriving in procession at the house of the girl's father, the messengers demanded the bride, and the surprise and shock to her parents when they heard of their daughter's disappearance was as though the heavens had fallen. They saw at once what had happened—how they had been imposed upon, and their daughter stolen by some rogues.

Fearing a scene, and perhaps a scandal, they then and there invented a story to get rid of the party.

"Alas!" said they, "our daughter is dead; the long neglect of her husband caused her to die of a broken heart;" and with that they actually began to beat their breasts and tear their hair, as if their sorrow had welled up afresh at the recollection of her death.

The party returned sorrowfully, and broke the sad news of the reported death of the girl to her husband.

The latter was beside himself with grief, and repented of his past neglect; but it was now, as he thought, too late to repair the wrong he had done, and his parents, hoping to relieve his sorrow, thought of replacing a wife by a wife, just as a thorn removes the pain of a thorn. A fresh marriage was accordingly arranged, and the wedding day fixed.

To the wooden maid was entrusted the duty of getting a wedding-suit and seeing that a pair of shoes was made for the bridegroom, her master. She went to a tailor. "Mr. Tailor," said she, addressing him, "be pleased to make a wedding suit for my master, but do not forget, the trousers are to have but one leg and the coat but one sleeve."

An order is an order, and the tailor did not trouble himself about the eccentricities of his customers, so he made the suit exactly as it had been ordered.

Next she went to a shoemaker and said to him: "Mr. Shoemaker, be pleased to make a pair of shoes, each of a different colour." This order, too, was carried out exactly as it was given.

The tailor delivered the suit to the employer of the Wooden Maid, but when he saw the one-legged trousers and one-sleeved coat he was furious, and asked what the tailor meant by it.

"Sir," said the tailor, "I am not to blame. I have made the suit exactly as it was ordered by the Wooden Maid."

So the Wooden Maid was sent for, and, when she

came, was asked whether she had given such an absurd order.

"Maybe I did, but I cannot say for certain," said she. "Thou seest mine is a wooden tongue, so it might not have given the order exactly as a real flesh-and-blood tongue would have done."

Next came the shoemaker with the shoes, each of a different colour, and the cobbler was taken to task in the same way as the tailor had been, but he too put the blame on the Wooden Maid.

She was again asked whether she had given the blundering order.

"Maybe I did, but I cannot say for certain," said the Wooden Maid. "Thou seest mine is a wooden tongue, so it might not have given the order exactly as a real flesh-and-blood tongue would have done."

As the wedding suit and shoes had been delivered, according to the instructions of the Wooden Maid, on the wedding day, there was no time to order others, and so, dressed in the one-legged trousers and one-sleeved coat, with a different coloured shoe on each foot, the bridegroom went forth to the house of the bride; but his prospective father-in-law, seeing him appear dressed more like a madman than a bridegroom, refused to marry his daughter to him.

The party had nothing else to do but return the way they went, and the bridegroom, looking upon the Wooden Maid as the cause of all this mischief, determined to punish her.

As soon as the Wooden Maid saw the wedding party returning without the bride, she began to laugh in her wooden sleeve. At this her master, intending to wreak his vengeance upon her, rushed up and shook her violently, when off fell the disguise, and his own long-neglected wife, supposed to be dead, suddenly stood before him in all the loveliness of life.

Thus were the husband and wife reunited, and lived long and happily together.

THE LUCKY MOUSTACHE.

ONCE upon a time an unlettered but cunning Brahmin took up his residence in a village of cowherds. He could not read his Scriptures, even backwards like the devil, but all the same he soon came to be regarded as a prodigy of learning in the eyes of his neighbours. Indeed, what he lacked in the way of learning was made up for by the loudness of his speech, and his "words of learned length and thundering sound" did duty admirably for scholarship for a time. He had an ingenious way of putting catchy questions to every stray pundit he came across, and invariably succeeded in tripping him up; but it was not long before he met his match in the person of another Brahmin, as unlettered as himself, but apparently shrewder.

One day the latter happened to pass through the village, and the favourite of the cowherds pounced upon him and at once started an argument. The cowherds gathered round with as much interest as if they were going to witness a ram-fight. They encouraged their favourite by a loud clapping of hands, as he stepped in front of his rival and asked him the meaning and origin of "Gan-Gor-Gour."

His adversary scratched his bald head for a moment, and then made this answer:

"At sunset," he thus began, "when the lowing herds return from the fields through a golden haze of dust raised by their hoofs, the calves are let loose, and the cows are milked. At first, as the milk drops into the empty pails, it makes the sound of 'chun-bhun, chun-bhun,' but, directly the pails become fuller, the sound changes to 'Gan-Gor-Gour, Gan-Gor-Gour.' Is not that so?" asked this pundit, turning round to the cowherds for corroboration. "That's right, that's right," they shouted.

In this way was the favourite of the cowherds humiliated at the hands of his despised rival, and the latter, not content with his victory, rushed up to his adversary and plucked out seven hairs from his moustache. At this outrage on their old favourite, the assembled cowherds threatened to assault him, but, with wonderful presence of mind, he found a way out of his difficulties. "You see," said he, "there is luck in every hair of his moustache. Whoever gets one will have good fortune."

No sooner had he spoken the words than all the cowherds began to pluck out hairs from the unfortunate man's moustache. Soon it disappeared altogether, and their erstwhile favourite lay senseless on the ground. One man, however, did not arrive in time to secure one of the lucky hairs, and his wife scolded him, saying, "Where have you been? Everyone else has had their share of good luck but you." Without waiting to hear more, he ran straight to the new champion and said, "Oh, sir, save for the moustache and the tuft of hair on his head, our Brahmin was clean shaven, and now there is not a single hair of his moustache left for me. What shall I have for good luck?"

"Well," replied the hero of the contest, "as the hair on his head is still left, it will bring as good luck as any other."

Overjoyed at the news, the cowherd tore off the wretched man's top-knot without more ado, and in triumph carried it home to his wife.

After this, the cowherds gathered round their old favourite, who was still lying unconscious on the ground, and laid their heads together to devise some means of bringing him back to his senses. Seeing this, and anxious to make his victory still more complete, the stranger said: "What are you in the habit of doing when your bullocks are in this condition and you wish them to get up?" "Why, we put a red-hot iron to their heads," replied all the cowherds with one voice. "That, then," said he, "is exactly what you ought to do now."

No sooner did they hear this than they actually applied, in the same manner as they were accustomed to do to their cattle, a hot iron to the temples of the unconscious man. As soon as he felt the iron, the poor wretch cried out with pain, and, sitting up with a start, put his hand where his top-knot had been, in his efforts to allay the pain. The cowherds, suddenly struck with the idea that the red-hot iron should have been applied to that part of the head instead of to the temples, put it there.

The Brahmin, smarting under this new pain, sprang to his feet and bolted out of the village as fast as his legs could carry him, and never again played the pundit in his life. His victorious rival was installed in his place.

THE FLUTES OF FORTUNE AND MISFORTUNE.

ONCE upon a time there was a little orphan boy, who, though loved by his elder brother, was hated by his sister-in-law. She made him earn his keep by tending their cattle. Yet, for all his trouble, he never had enough to eat, and every night went hungry to bed. As a result, he gradually grew weaker and weaker until the time came when he was no longer able to run after the cattle and prevent them from straying into other people's fields. So it befell that he used to be beaten every day by the owners of the fields which had been damaged.

One day, after having been beaten by one of these men, he sat down under a tree and began to weep, when a beautiful cow came up to him and enquired why he was weeping. The boy told her his tale of woe, whereupon the cow said: "Know me, O boy! to be the Wishing-Cow (Kam-Dhenu) of Indra. For your sake I shall remain with your brother's cattle, and help you out of your misery. I yield a never-ending supply of milk. You can live on it and give me your wretched crust of bread in exchange." This was agreed to, and the lad used to drink Kam-Dhenu's milk and feed her in return on his bread. By degrees he regained his former strength, and his skeleton filled out with flesh and blood. This attracted the notice of his sister-in-law. She thought he had been drinking the milk of her cows, and, though she had no proof of it, yet out of spite she sold off all her cattle so that he might be reduced again to his former half-starved condition. So all the cows, including Kam-Dhenu, were sold to a butcher; but, when the buyer came to take her away, she broke her rope and bolted, and her example was followed by all the other cows. The boy ran after Kam-Dhenu, and, catching hold of her tail, was dragged away clinging to it.

When Kam-Dhenu came down from heaven she had not come alone, but had brought with her other cows belonging to Indra, and these were wont to graze on the bank of a river. She now ran straight to her companions and introduced the boy to them. The latter now devoted all his time to tending the divine cows, and soon became a great favourite with them.

Close to where the sacred cows used to graze, there happened to be a big hole leading down into the underworld, where dwelt Vasuki, the King of the Snakes. One day, whilst standing near it, Kam-Dhenu said to the boy: "Drink as much of my milk as you can, but take care to fill an earthen jar to the brim with what is left and leave it at the mouth of the hole each day." This the boy did, and the King of the Snakes used to come out of the hole and drink the milk at night. He was much pleased with the boy's attention, and asked him how he could reward him for his services. The boy consulted Kam-Dhenu as to what he should ask for, and was advised to request that a golden comb, a golden cot, and the Flutes of Fortune and Misfortune might be given to him.

The King of the Snakes presented the boy with the things he named, and sent him away rejoicing.

He had not, however, been told the use of the flutes, and, as he blew the one when he ought to have blown the other, all the cows came running back from the pastures before the usual time, thinking that something untoward had happened, for the boy had blown the Flute of Misfortune.

Kam-Dhenu soon found out what had happened, and, fearing lest the other cows should be angry with the boy for having brought them back unnecessarily from the fields, instructed him in the use of the flutes, that is, as to which flute should be blown and when, and told him to blow the Flute of Fortune at once. As soon as this was done, the cows went back to the pastures, leaving the boy unmolested.

The boy used now to blow the Flute of Fortune at dawn, when the cows would go peacefully to their pastures, and that of Misfortune at dusk, when they would return gloomily to their folds. In this way time went on until one day the boy, now grown up into a youth, went down to the river for a bathe ; after that he changed his clothes and was combing his hair with the golden comb which was presented to him by the King of the Snakes, when, strange to relate, all his hair became golden. A few loose hairs, however, came out, and these he put, coiled, inside a cup of leaves, and set it afloat on the stream.

Down the stream floated the cup, and it so happened that the King's daughter, who happened to be bathing in the river, saw it floating towards her. She at once stretched out her hand and drew it towards her, when what was her surprise to find the golden hairs! Straightway she fell in love with the unknown from whose head they had come.

Quite overcome by her feelings, the young Princess shut herself up and refused to touch either food or drink. The Queen looked for her all over the palace, and was surprised to find her in her room in an extremely agitated state.

"If anyone has cast evil looks upon you," said she, "I will have his eyes gouged out. If anybody has spoken rudely to you, I will have his tongue burnt out. If anyone has raised his hand against you, I will have it cut off. If anyone has raised his foot against you, I will have it taken off."

"None has cast evil looks on me, or has spoken rudely to me or has attempted to raise hand or foot against me," said the young Princess. She then brought out the golden hairs, and, showing them to her mother, said: "Oh, mother, if you do not get me married to the owner of these hairs, I will never leave this room, and will touch neither food nor drink."

The Queen felt extremely anxious about her daughter, so, to please her, she sent the royal barber immediately to find the golden-haired one. The barber set out on the errand with a heavy heart, for he did not know where to look for him; but, after a long search, he at last succeeded in discovering the youth with the golden hair, seated on a golden cot which hung from the branches of a gigantic banyan-tree. The orphan boy, for it was he, thinking that the barber had come to crop his golden hair, at once blew the Flute of Misfortune, and immediately all the cows returned from the pastures and went straight for the barber with their horns lowered. The barber escaped with his life by running his fastest, and the golden-haired boy, with a blast on the Flute of Fortune, sent all the cows back again.

Utterly discomfited, the barber returned home and reported his failure to the Queen, who again sent him, this time with a powerful elephant, to capture the youth with the golden hair. Returning to the spot where the boy lay suspended from the branches of the banyan-tree, the elephant raised its trunk to seize hold of him; but quick as lightning the youth climbed higher up the tree and blew a blast on the Flute of Misfortune, when in the twinkling of an eye all the cows rushed back from the pastures and attacked the elephant in front, flank, and rear, almost goring him to death. The elephant, with the barber on its back, at once stampeded, bleeding and bellowing with pain.

The Queen, nothing daunted, bethought her of a more ingenious plan. She trained a parrot to steal flutes, and once more sent the barber, this time with the parrot, to the golden-haired youth. He found him seated on his golden cot, hung between two branches of the tree, as on the two previous occasions. Below him on the ground was a bowl of milk with a piece of cloth over it. The parrot at once perched on it, and, as the cloth dipped in the milk, began to drink it. The golden-haired youth clapped his hands to frighten it away, and, failing to do so, he threw one of the flutes, which happened to be the Flute of Misfortune, at it. The parrot at once snatched it up in his beak and flew away with it to the Queen.

The latter, overjoyed at getting the flute, blew it, when, ere long, the palace was surrounded by an infuriated herd of cattle, which began to dig their horns into the walls, and soon made the whole palace shake as if with an earthquake.

The King, almost frightened out of his wits, immediately despatched a messenger to the golden-haired youth, promising to give his daughter in marriage to him, and half the kingdom as her dowry, if he would only come and pacify the cows. The offer proved too tempting for the youth to refuse. He came and blew the Flute of Fortune, when the cows at once returned to the pastures. Amidst great rejoicings, the youth was married to the Princess, and all promised to go well. But one night, while the Princess lay asleep, a serpent crawled up her hair, which was hanging down to the ground, bit the Prince, and hid itself inside his nose. The next morning the Prince was found stone-dead on his bed, and all the cows, headed by Kam-Dhenu, waited long in front of the palace for the usual summons from the flute. They waited and waited, but no sound came from the Flute of Fortune, and, at last, the sad news of the death of their favourite by snake-bite was broken to them. Kam-Dhenu straightway went to the King of the Snakes and thus said to him: "Oh, Vasuki, the youth who fed and cared for you so long has been killed by one of your own serpents."

The King of the Snakes became very angry, and. accompanying Kam-Dhenu to the palace, ordered the offending snake to come out of the Prince's nose, and suck out the poison he had injected into his body. This was done as commanded, and the youth sat up on his bed as if he had just awoke from his sleep, and lived with his bride happily ever after.

THE SAND-RIVER, THE STONE-BOAT, AND THE MONKEY-FERRYMAN.

ONCE upon a time there was a King who was fond of surrounding himself with beautiful objects. He had surrounded his palace with a charming park and lake, and, to make everything perfect, he longed for a certain pair of divine swans to settle on the lake and float majestically on the water.

Far away on an island, amidst the seven seas which encircle the world, lived this pair of swans. "If I can get the swans," thought the King, "and see them swimming on the lake, its beauty will be enhanced a hundred-fold. But alas! seas have to be crossed, and the task is beset with perils."

Next morning the King, calling together all his sons, said to them: "My dear sons, I have decorated my palace with a beautiful lake, but its beauty is not complete without swans. Now there is a pair of divine swans, far exceeding in loveliness any swans which are met with on earth, and they inhabit a far-away island, somewhere amidst the seven seas which encircle the earth. Whichever of you shall fetch me the pair shall have half my kingdom for reward."

Of his three sons the two elder ones leapt up joyfully, and, binding their swords to their girdles, set off at once in quest of the swans. They took the road seawards, but on the way they had to encounter a wily magician. He was able, by his magic, to make a river of sand, on which a monkey was made to ply a boat hollowed out of stone. If any unwary traveller witnessed the strange occurrence, he naturally told it to the next man he came across, and the magician always arranged to be the first to meet him. The traveller would tell him what he had seen, and the magician would lay a wager with him, saying: "If what you say is found to be false, you must become my slave, but, if otherwise, I shall be yours."

The traveller, trusting to his eyes, would naturally accept the challenge, and then the magician would raise a dust storm, and as soon as that subsided, lo and behold! there remained no trace of the sand-river, the stone-boat, or the monkey-ferryman.

In this way many a traveller had lost his liberty and become the slave of the magician. The two young Princes were no exception to the rule, and they too fell into the snare and became the slaves of the magician.

A long time elapsed, and yet they did not return with the swans, and the King then sent forth his youngest son, their step-brother, on the same errand. He, too, set out on the quest for the swans, wearing on his finger a magic ring which his mother had given him. Now this ring had the power of making whoever looked on it claim kinship with the wearer. Thus equipped, he journeyed the whole day until the shades of evening fell, and then began to look for a shelter. Soon he saw a palatial mansion, apparently unoccupied, with its gates wide open, standing out against the grey twilight sky, whilst in the background was a large forest. He walked boldly in through the gates, and, entering the mansion, began to explore all the rooms, when what was his amazement to find in one of them a Princess all alone! Still greater was his astonishment when, so far from resenting his presence, she welcomed him, and claimed him as her cousin, for she had looked on the ring on his finger.

The Princess proved to be the only survivor of the royal family, which had lived in the palace until a giant came, ate up all her kinsfolk, and made it his home. She alone was saved, for she had awakened in the giant a feeling of affection, and was being brought up as if she were his daughter. At candle-light the giant returned home with the motion of a hurricane and with strides as long as the distance between the stars, and, as he entered the house, began to sniff about him, saying,

"How Mow Khow
I smell human flesh now."

The Princess, holding the stranger by the hand, introduced him to the giant as her cousin, and the giant, seeing the magic ring, at once owned kinship with him. He became as mild as a lamb, and said, "How do you do, my nephew? You are welcome here."

The Princess was fast growing up into womanhood, and the giant was anxious to get her married. He took a fancy to the Prince and married the Princess to him. The Prince walked round the altar of fire and took six steps with his bride instead of the usual seven which complete the marriage, saying that he would reserve the seventh step until the time of his return to his own country. He told the giant of the errand on which his father had sent him, and the dangers likely to be encountered on the way. "If I die in the course of my adventure," said he, "your daughter will be free to marry again, and for this reason I purposely refrained from taking the seventh step, and thus left the marriage incomplete. If, however, I succeed in my adventure, I will come back, complete the marriage, and take my bride home."

The giant was greatly pleased with the Prince's solicitude for his daughter, and blessed his adventure. He also took care to warn him of the wily magician, and, to enable him to checkmate him, provided him with a magic lamp, telling him that if he kept the lamp concealed on his person the magician would not be able to impose upon him. He also gave him a magic horse and a magic whip. The magic horse would carry anyone over land or sea or through the air to whatever place its rider might wish, while the magic whip had the power of making whomsoever it touched yield and do the bidding of him who held it.

The Prince, having expressed his gratitude for the gifts, took leave of the giant, and rode away on the magic horse to the island. No sooner had he landed there than a fearful monster appeared before him, and barred his way; but he laid the magic whip vigorously about him, and the monster at once crouched at his feet like a kitten, and stood awaiting commands. The Prince then ordered him to deliver up the pair of divine swans which lived on the island, and this was no sooner said than done.

Taking possession of the swans, the Prince quickly mounted his horse and rode away to seek his brothers. At last he came to the spot where the magician lived, and went up to him. The magician looked at him through his half-closed eyes with some misgiving, and, setting his heart on the beautiful swans, tried to entrap him as he had done many an unwary traveller before. The magician at once got into conversation with him regarding the sand-river, the stone-boat, and the monkey-ferryman, but the Prince only made fun of it all, and upon that the magician became angry and asked him to have a wager on it. The terms of the wager were that whoever of the two was wrong must agree to be the slave of the other. The Prince agreed to the conditions, and the magician thereupon took him to show him the sand-river, the stone-boat and the monkey-ferryman; but lo and behold! there was neither the one nor the other. His magic powers had failed owing to the lamp which the Prince carried with him, and, instead of a sand-river, there flowed a crystal stream, and so the magician lost his wager, and became the Prince's slave.

Now all a slave's possessions are his master's, and so the Prince became the owner of all that belonged to the magician, his slaves as well as his worldly goods. He set free the slaves, and among them his two elder step-brothers. The magician was delivered over into the charge of his former servants, and the Prince, accompanied by the brothers, set off for the house of his giant father-in-law with the swans. Arrived there, he completed the marriage with the Princess and took leave of his father-in-law, who presented him on his departure with the magic frying-pan as part of the dowry. Now this frying-pan had the wonderful property of supplying ready-cooked whatever its owner wished to eat, and so with it and the magic horse, lamp, and whip the Prince was well equipped.

Accompanied by his brothers and his bride, together with the swans and the magic pan, the Prince started on the magic horse for his own country; but on the way it grew dark, and, the brothers feigning hunger and thirst, the party alighted from the horse, and, sitting down by a well, partook of a sumptuous dinner from the magic frying-pan. After it was over, the Prince bent down to draw water for the party, when one of his brothers, envious of his good-luck, cut off his head with one stroke of his sword, the trunk turning right over and falling into the well in a standing posture, with the legs apart and pressing against the sides of the well, while the head was snapped up by a flying Peri. The brothers then proceeded to seize the magic horse, the Princess, and the swans; but away flew the swans and the horse, with the Princess on its back, into the air, and kept hovering over the well, the scene of the tragedy.

Balked of their prey, the brothers had nothing left but to return home with empty hands.

At day-break a traveller came to the well, and, lowering his rope to draw some water, saw to his horror a headless body. Scared out of his senses, he did not dare to take a second look, but flew from the place as fast as his legs would carry him.

Soon afterwards there came rustling through the air a Peri, carrying a head in one hand and a bowl of ambrosia in the other. She lifted the body out of the well, and, putting the head on to it, brought it back to life by sprinkling some ambrosia on it, and then flew away.

The Prince got up with a start, as if he had been awakened from his sleep, and at the same moment the horse, the Princess, and the swans came down from the air above, and all five started off again. The Prince, thanks to his magic horse, reached home long before his brothers, and presented the divine swans to his father. He also told him how he had found his brothers working as the slaves of a magician, of their rescue by him, and of their ingratitude, and his other adventures.

The King at once ordered three holes to be made, and, when his two wicked sons returned home, he had them buried, each in one hole and their mother in the third, since there was no knowing what she might do in revenge for the death of her sons.

He set the swans free on his lake, and used to feed them on pearls every day. Thus was the dream of his life realised, and, according to his promise, both father and son ruled the kingdom happily together.

THE MONKEY GIANT-KILLER.

ONCE upon a time a traveller, feeling hungry, threw down his bundle under a shady tree and ran to the nearest wayside well for a cup of water. He took off his much-folded turban, and, tying one end of it round the neck of the vessel, let it down into the well and pulled it out by the other end; for various indeed are the uses of turbans to travellers.

With the cup full of water he returned to the place where he had left his bundle, but to his horror he found it lying open, and his bread gone! Looking up into the tree, he saw, on a top-branch, a sturdy monkey munching a mouthful of fried peas out of a small earthen pot, which had evidently been pilfered but a short while before from some unlucky passer-by.

"Sir Monkey," said the traveller, addressing the monkey, "wilt thou take pity on me and share thy peas with me? I am dying of hunger."

The monkey had his mouth too full of peas to reply, so, carrying the pot under his left arm, with his fist thrust into its mouth so as to keep the contents from falling out, he leapt from bough to bough, and came down to the ground and shared the peas with the traveller. After that, the latter thanked the monkey and got up to go.

"Sir Traveller," said the monkey, "why art thou in such great haste to get away with my peas inside thee?"

"Sir Monkey," replied the traveller, taken aback by the strange demand, "I have been tramping the earth, and must be off home now. Thou canst not both give me thy peas and keep them too. How can I return them to thee?"

"I do not care how," replied the monkey, "but, Sir Traveller, my peas must be returned before thou budgest an inch from here, or else thou must carry me on thy shoulders wherever I care to go."

The traveller had no alternative but to submit to his terms, and the monkey, mounting on his shoulders, rode him about, this way and that, using his ears for reins and his own tail for a whip, now turning him to the left by pulling his left ear, and now to the right by pulling his right ear.

Before they had gone far they met a drummer.

"Sir Traveller," said the monkey, "I must have this drum or my peas back."

The traveller bought him the drum. A little way further on, the monkey, seeing an old woman by the road-side, separating the chaff from the wheat with a large winnowing-fan, again demanded this of the traveller, who perforce had to get it for him also, for, of course, he could not return the wretched peas. In this way, too, the monkey later on possessed himself of a long coiled-up rope, resembling in shape the folds of a snake.

By this time it was growing dark and night was near, so the natural instincts of the monkey bade him make for the nearest wood. Arrived there, he found a mansion showing no signs of life, and with its gates closed. Overhanging the house was a tall tree, and into it the monkey climbed, with the traveller clinging to his tail, and from its branches both managed to clamber on to the roof of the house.

On looking through the skylight, they saw to their amazement a huge giantess snoring, with a charming maiden sleeping by her side ; and the traveller trembled from head to foot, fearing that the giantess might wake from her sleep and eat him up.

The monkey now said he felt thirsty, and asked the traveller to pass him the brass cup with some water in it. The traveller implored him to keep quiet, lest the giantess should be awakened by the noise, but the monkey insisted, saying : "Thou must either pass me the cup or let me have my peas back."

The traveller brought the cup on tip-toe, and the monkey at once drank half its contents, and then poured out what was left through the skylight over the head of the sleeping giantess. With a grunt she sat up on the edge of her bed and looked up towards the skylight. She seemed to think that it had been raining, and quickly lay down to sleep again ; but no sooner had she done so than thud ! came the cup against her head, hurled by the monkey with all the strength at his command. At this, fearing that the end had come, the traveller swooned away from sheer fright.

The giantess looked up, but could see nothing but a monster's head grinning at her, and at once jumped out of bed to fight him. The monkey, guessing her intention, threw down the rope to her, saying : "Dost thou want to fight me ? Look ! here is my tail," pointing to the rope, "I am a bigger giant than thou art."

The giantess was evidently puzzled, and perhaps a little frightened into the bargain, but, before she could say anything, he threw down the winnowing-fan, saying: "Dost thou doubt that? Here is one of my ears," and with that he jumped down from the roof, beating the drum loudly as if he were going to fight her.

The giantess, taking the monkey at his word, and believing him to be bigger than she was, bolted out of the house for her life, closely pursued by the monkey, drumming and biting at the calves of her legs. Not seeing where she was going in the dark, she tumbled down into a well, head foremost, and was killed.

The monkey then ran back to the house, and, finding the traveller still in a swoon, pulled him by the ears till he came to his senses, and told him what had happened.

Both of them then went in to the house and found the maiden unconscious on her bed, apparently through fright The monkey now bethought him of a different method to revive her, and instead of pulling her ears, as he had done to the traveller, he kissed her on her rosy cheeks with his clammy lips. Presently the maiden sat up screaming, but, seeing that a human being of flesh and blood like herself was with the monkey, and hearing of the death of the giantess, she soon recovered her senses.

After this the traveller, the monkey, and the maiden soon became friends, and the maiden was surprised to find that the traveller was no less a person than a Prince in disguise. The traveller on his side was no less amazed when he heard that the lovely figure before him was a Princess, the only one of her family spared by the giantess.

The Prince married the Princess, and ruled over his State, while the wise monkey, in reward for all he had done for both, was well cared for, and all three lived long and happily together.

THE GOLDEN CALF.

ONCE upon a time there was a certain rich man, but as time went on he became poor. He did not, however, long survive his poverty, but died, leaving behind him two orphan boys utterly unprovided for.

Thus suddenly turned adrift into the world, they were at a loss to know what to do for a livelihood; so, selling off what was left of their home, they decided to go to a foreign land in the hope of making a living there.

So it befell that one day, under cover of darkness, just before dawn, they left their home; but, not being accustomed to long journeys on foot, they had not gone far before they became tired and hungry. In front, behind, and around them, there stretched field after field, as far as the eye could see, and nothing did they find to eat but some peas, which, luckily for them, grew in one of the fields. They ate as many of them as they could, and then took some with them to feed them on the way. They then went to drink water at a river close by, and there they found a golden-hued bull-calf standing with his legs stretched wide apart, and drinking water. The elder brother wanted to wait until the calf had finished, but the younger brother was not so patient, and pushed the calf aside to make room for himself, whereupon the animal started bellowing, "Humba, Humba!" as loudly as if he had been seized by a tiger; and the brothers, fearing lest the cry should attract the owner of the pea-field to the spot, and cause their theft to be discovered, tried to appease the calf and entreated him to keep quiet.

"If you promise to take me with you," said the calf to the younger brother, "and share your food with me, then only shall I cease crying."

To this he had to agree, and the brothers started off again, taking the calf with them.

On and on they journeyed until the shades of evening fell, when they sought shelter with a family for the night, and the brothers, borrowing a mortar and pestle, crushed the peas, and made themselves two cakes. They then sat down to their dinner without, however, inviting the calf, but the latter, according to the compact, ate half the younger brother's cake. Now the head of the family which had given them shelter took pity on them, and employed them to look after his cattle. Every day the golden calf used to accompany the cattle to the pastures with the two brothers and have his meals with the younger one.

As time went on, the youths managed to put by enough against a rainy day, and it was the elder brother who kept the money for both. As their circumstances had improved, their employer decided to give his daughter in marriage to the elder of the two. Verily this marriage was the beginning of fresh troubles for the younger brother, for his sister-in-law soon came to hate him, and planned to rob him of his share of the savings.

So after this, one day when her husband was ill at home, she took the cattle to graze with her brother-in-law, and, while they were feeding, she went and sat by him and pretended to smooth down his ruffled hair.

While she was thus engaged he began to doze, and then the wicked woman, taking out a sharp knife from under her clothes, cut his head off at one stroke. After that, she buried the head in one place and the body in another, and then returned home with the cattle.

The golden calf, however, not seeing his master, became very anxious, and began to search for him all over the fields. Then, suddenly noticing marks of blood and following them up, he at last succeeded in finding the head in one place and the body in another. He was not, however, an ordinary calf, but was acquainted with the virtues of herbs, so, putting the head on to the body and then applying the juice of a certain herb he knew of, he brought the younger brother back to life, and the latter, as he got up to go, exclaimed: "What, have I been sleeping too long? It has got quite dark."

They returned home together, and naturally his sister-in-law was frightened almost out of her wits to see her dead brother-in-law come back, restored to life. This, she rightly guessed, was the work of the calf, so she planned to get rid of him first. Filled with evil designs, she went to her bed at once, pretending to be ill, and, when her husband enquired what was the matter with her (for she had cooked nothing for him and his brother), she said: "I have a very bad headache. I consulted an astrologer, and he advised me to bathe my head in the blood of the golden calf, if I wanted to be cured of it soon," with a significant stress on the last word.

Her husband, dreading the idea of having either to go starving or do the cooking for the family, at once sent for a butcher, and, fetching the calf, said to him: "An astrologer has told my wife to cure her headache by bathing her head in the blood of this calf, so take him away, slaughter him, and bring me his blood."

"The astrologer wants my blood," said the calf to the butcher, "but not my flesh, so see to it you do not put your knife into my flesh."

"How can I get the blood without cutting the flesh?" cried the butcher, frightened. "I cannot do the impossible."

So back went the husband to his wife and informed her of what had passed between the calf and the butcher.

When she heard it she said angrily: "Go and tell the butcher, a few pieces of flesh mixed with the blood will not matter."

He told him, but the calf again warned the butcher: "Very well," said he, "you can have my flesh and blood if you like, but mind you do not touch my bones. The astrologer said nothing of them."

Back went the husband to his wife and repeated the words to her. She cried out: "All this silly nonsense has made my headache worse. Go and get me both his blood, flesh, and bones, if you please. I will have no more excuses."

The calf, finding it impossible to ward off his doom, went to take leave of the younger brother, to whom he told everything. Between them they planned a way of escape. "Do thou pretend to take me to thy elder brother," said the calf, "and on the way I will manage to run away from thee, and then thou must follow me as if to capture me. When we have got out of thy brother's sight, spring on my back. I will then carry thee to an island inhabited by Peris (fairies) far away from these wicked people, but, should I die, do not mourn for me, but secretly watch what happens to my body. You will see a number of Peris swoop down from above to eat my flesh, but, directly they find it is the dead body of a calf, they will go away without tasting it. Next will come a Gorur (a divine eagle). Catch him if you can, and, when you have caught him, say to him: 'Oh, wicked bird, thou hast killed my calf; either give thy daughter in marriage to me or I will kill thee. If he agrees to do this, take care to make him swear it three times."

In accordance with this plan, the younger brother acted out the little drama. He dragged the calf, who feigned unwillingness, before his elder brother, when, as previously arranged, the calf broke loose and bolted, followed by the younger brother, and so both of them escaped.

The calf never stopped until he reached the island, having leapt over the seas, but, when he arrived there, he dropped down dead from sheer exhaustion.

The younger brother did as he had been bid by the calf before his death, and, true enough, a band of Peris came flying through the air; but, when they found the dead body to be that of a calf, they flew away without tasting it.

Next came a Gorur, as predicted, and the younger brother sprang upon him and caught him. "Thou hast killed my calf," said he to the bird, "and I will kill thee unless thou givest thy daughter in marriage to me."

The bird had no alternative but to submit to the terms of his captor, and, fetching his daughter before him, laconically introduced them to each other, saying, "Here is thy bridegroom, and here is thy bride."

"A daughter and a cow," said the bride, "are alike. They become another's property by gift. They have no choice of their own."

Handing over his daughter to his son-in-law, the Gorur said: "The father supports his daughter until her marriage. Now rests on thee the duty of maintaining thy wife." The Gorur then blessed the couple, and, taking leave of them, flew away.

The Gorur's daughter, who could, with eagle-eyed clearness, see into the past, the present, and the future, had little difficulty in discovering her husband to be a wandering vagabond without the wherewithal to maintain a wife. With tears streaming down her cheeks, she went down to the river and prayed to Vishnu, the god of her tribe, either to build her and her husband a suitable habitation and give them enough to eat and drink for the rest of their lives, or else to let her drown herself, and so put an end to her life; and lo! in answer to her prayer there arose before their admiring eyes an imposing house, filled with enough food to last them a lifetime.

The couple at once took possession of the house and for a time lived happily, but alas! the course of true love seldom runs smooth. The Gorur's daughter possessed the fatal gift of beauty, and this brought on her a series of misfortunes.

One day it so happened that, while the Gorur's daughter, who had just taken a bath, was sitting out in the sun drying her golden hair, a colt, which had got loose from the stables of the King of the island, found its way into her house, and she hunted it away, giving it a slap over its brow, where she left the impression of her five golden fingers.

The colt ran back home, and the King, noticing the five golden finger-marks upon its brow, guessed its assailant to be a lady of uncommon beauty, and straightway felt a keen desire to see her. The King sent for the royal barber at once, and, when he came, pointed to the five golden finger-marks on the colt's forehead, and thus said to him: "O barber! thou match-maker and go-between of Princes, thou must secure the fair one who has struck my colt, to be my Queen."

The barber soon found the Gorur's daughter and asked her if she had slapped the King's colt.

She did not deny it, and back went the barber to the King with the good news of the discovery of his colt's assailant.

"Thou canst not win the affections of the lady," said the sharp-witted barber, "until thou gettest rid of her husband. She is a goddess in beauty, and deserves to be thy Queen."

Thereupon the King had the husband of the Gorur's daughter brought before him, and thus addressed him: "I do not know who thou art, but thy wife has committed treason by striking my colt, for beating my colt is the same thing as beating me. For this thou and thy wife deserve severe punishment. I can, however, pardon thee and thy wife on one condition only, and that is, if thou canst successfully carry out three successive tasks which I shall impose on thee."

Finding himself in this predicament, the husband asked the King to tell him at once what his first task was to be.

The King then ordered a hundred-weight of mustard seed, each seed as tiny as the head of a pin, to be scattered over a ploughed-up field, and, when that was done, he turned to the Gorur's son-in-law and said to him: "Here is thy first task. Do thou collect the seeds, one by one, during the night and fetch them before me at dawn on the morrow. If the seeds weigh a hundred-weight, neither more nor less by a single grain, then I shall impose my second task upon thee, but, shouldst thou fail, thy life shall be forfeit."

With a heavy heart, the Gorur's son-in-law went home to his wife and told her of all that had passed between the King and himself, and asked her advice as to how to accomplish the first task he had been given.

"Do not be anxious, dear," said his wife, "thou knowest that my father is the King of birds, and all the birds of the forest, at his command, will come and pick the seeds up and collect them into a sack." She then informed her father of everything, and asked for his assistance on behalf of her husband.

In the twinkling of an eye, all the birds of the world came flocking to the field, and picked up all the seeds overnight, but the King of the birds found one tiny little grain missing. He took the birds to task for it, but, after they had all protested their innocence, he searched them one and all, when lo! the missing seed was found concealed in the blind eye of one of them.

He was punished, all the other birds attacking him with their beaks and claws.

At dawn on the following morning, the hundred-weight of seed was produced before the King, and an army of royal auditors and accountants were busy all day counting up the seeds, and, wonder of wonders! they were found to be exactly correct in number and weight.

The first task having been accomplished, the King called the barber before him, and, telling him that the first task had been successfully performed, asked him what the next task should be. The barber scratched his head for a minute, and then out came this ingenious suggestion: "Thy Majesty," said he, nothing daunted, "canst now ask the husband of the fair lady to fetch thee a bowl of tigress's milk. Of course, he will be eaten up by the tigress in the attempt to get her milk, and then the lady shall be thine."

Accordingly, the King told the Gorur's son-in-law to get him a bowl of tigress's milk, "or," he added, "thy life shall be forfeit."

Back went the latter to his wife and informed her of the second task the King had imposed upon him.

"Is that all, dear?" answered his wife. "Do not be anxious about it." And, saying this, she took off one of her rings, which was set with a bright stone, and, handing it to her husband, continued: "Go to the wood and hold the stone up towards the sun. There will be a flash of fire, and with that the forest will be set aflame. Then there will be a hurrying to and fro of the panic-stricken animals, but, if thou keepest watch, thou wilt see tigresses running away, leaving their cubs behind. The cubs will make for a place of safety, and do thou follow them with a quantity of pepul figs in thy pockets. Then climb up into a tree and keep throwing the fruits to the cubs. They will come up to the foot of the tree and look towards thee for more. Their mother is sure to trace them out sooner or later, and, finding that thou hast well cared for them, is sure to reward thee. Thou canst then ask for her milk."

The Gorur's son-in-law did as he was bid, and the tigress, pleased with him, not only gave him a bowl full of her milk, but also one of her cubs, a full-grown one, lest the King should think that a fraud had been practised upon him.

After that, while the King was holding a council, surrounded by his courtiers, in stepped the Gorur's son-in-law, attended by the cub, with a bowl of tigress's milk, and lo! there was a stampede among the people present, the King jumping down from the throne and running into the zenana, filled with fear. The Gorur's son-in-law, however, was told to leave the bowl of milk there and go away with the tiger, until he was again sent for by the King.

The King, having been assured that the Gorur's son-in-law was gone, at once sent for the barber. "Thou art a wicked barber," said he, with a burst of anger. "Thou hadst nearly brought about my death, for the husband of the accursed lady has been here, accompanied by a full-grown tiger."

The second attempt to get rid of him having failed, the barber was asked to suggest his next plan, and was warned, if it failed again, he would have to suffer death instead of his intended victim.

The barber racked his brain for a long while, and then with a chuckle unfolded his next piece of wickedness.

"Thy Majesty, there is now no way of escape for the man at all. Send him forth to heaven, saying: 'I want thee to go up to heaven and come back and tell me how my ancestors are faring there.' Of course, he will have to go the way they have gone to heaven, that is, through a funeral pyre, and will be surely reduced to ashes. Thus will the thorn in thy side be removed."

The King called the husband again, and this time asked him, as his last task, to go up to heaven to enquire after his ancestors.

"Thy Majesty," said he, "the journey to and back from heaven would take at least six months, and a large sum of money would be needed to keep my wife in comfort during my absence."

The King, only too willing to get rid of him, complied with his request, and asked him to get ready for heaven at once.

The Gorur's son-in-law went back to his wife, feeling sure of his doom, and the latter, on being told of it, took off another of her rings, set with a magic stone, and, handing it over to her husband, said: "Thou needest not fret over it, dear. Wear this ring on thy finger, and no fire can harm even a single hair of thy head. Leave the rest to me."

A funeral pyre was accordingly built up, just before dusk, and the Gorur's son-in-law sat upon it, quite as unconcerned as if he were sitting on his bridal couch. Around him a huge mass of wood was piled up to a great height, and the pyre was then set on fire. The wood blazed forth, the fire shooting into a hundred tongues, and the King and his courtiers, thinking all was over with him, went away.

The King, however, decided to wait the full six months before asking the man's widow to be his Queen, and so the lady was left unmolested.

In the meantime, after the King and his courtiers had gone, the woman went to the funeral pyre and secretly conveyed away her husband, who had not had a single hair singed, to an underground room which had been specially constructed for his hiding until the six months were past.

Every day the lady used to carry food and drink to her husband and tend him in his hiding place, and in this way the six months went by.

The Gorur's son-in-law had turned yellow from living so long under ground, deprived of fresh air and exercise, while his hair and nails had grown hideously long; so that, when the six months were up and he suddenly appeared before the King while he was holding court with all the fawning courtiers round him, there was the greatest consternation among the assembly, for they took him to be his own ghost, come back from hell to be revenged upon them.

However, after the first shock of surprise and fear was over, the King and his courtiers gathered round him, plying him with query after query regarding their ancestors.

"Thy Majesty," said the Gorur's son-in-law, "all thine ancestors are well and have sent thee their benediction by me; but one request they asked me to make of thee, before parting, and that is to send up thy royal barber to heaven at once. There are no barbers in heaven at all, and so their hair and nails have grown too long, just as mine have in six months. Further, they wished to reward me with a largesse of gold, but since there is no need of money in heaven, they want thee to pay me a handsome reward for them."

The King took him at his word and gave him a large reward, while, on the other hand, he ordered the barber to proceed at once to heaven, with razor and all, and the barber, caught in his own trap, ascended a funeral pyre and was soon reduced to cinders.

The King, however, turned over a new leaf, and, in compensation for all the harm he had sought to do the Gorur's son-in-law, appointed him his chief Minister, and he and his wife lived happily ever after.

THE WAGES OF SIN.

ONCE upon a time there was a certain merchant who had a large family of seven sons and one daughter. She was named Bija, and as might have been expected, was the darling of the whole family.

As time went on, she lost both her parents and became dependent upon her brothers. The brothers married, and their wives resented the presence of Bija in the family as if she were a thorn in their sides. Of course, they dared not express their hatred of her to their husbands, for the latter were fond of their sister, who in her turn was devotedly attached to them.

Concealing their hatred as best they could, the wicked women made Bija do all the domestic drudgery for them.

Bija put up with it all because she loved her brothers, and, for their sake at least, submitted to all the harsh commands of their wives without a grumble.

Unfortunately, however, for her, her brothers now had to go abroad on business, leaving the care of Bija to their wives.

Now the pent-up hatred of her sisters-in-law found a vent. They ordered Bija to go and get a bucket of water for them out of the well, at the same time forbidding her the use of any rope to draw it with, and threatening her with all sorts of punishment if she failed.

This was, of course, an impossible task, and Bija sat down by the well, and, beginning to sob and weep, kept saying to herself: "Alas! where are you, my dear brothers? Are you dead or alive? Why does Bija yet live in spite of the insults of her sisters-in-law?"

Attracted by her cries, a couple of crows came flying down to her and enquired the cause of her trouble. She told them of the task her wicked sisters-in-law had imposed upon her, and the crows flew down into the well and fetched water in their beaks and put it into the bucket, and thus by their joint and repeated efforts they at last succeeded in filling it with water to the brim.

Away went Bija to her sisters-in-law with the bucket full.

Next these cruel wretches laid their wicked heads together and devised another task for Bija.

They called her, and, giving her a quantity of unhusked paddy, ordered her to separate the husk from the grain without the help of mortar and pestle.

Bija went away with a heavy heart, and, spreading out the paddy in front of her, began to sob and weep. There was a tree close by where hundreds of mynas (finches) used to roost every night, and at dusk they came flying in a body to the tree.

Seeing the paddy spread out on the ground below, they flew down to eat it, but Bija said to herself: "Alas! where are you, my dear brothers? Are you dead or alive? Why does Bija yet live in spite of the insults of her sisters-in-law?" The birds, moved to pity, enquired the reason of her sadness.

Bija told them of the wickedness of her sisters-in-law, and of the impossible task which they had given her to do, and the mynas, making use of their beaks for mortar and pestle, separated the chaff from the corn in a trice.

Away went Bija to her sisters-in-law with the paddy husked and cleaned.

Again the wicked sisters devised another and still more difficult task for her—a task in the accomplishing of which she was, they thought, sure to perish. This time they asked her to go into the wood and fetch them the milk of the Akanda plant.[1] The wood was a great distance away by the side of a river, and was full of dangerous animals, and none dared to go there alone and unarmed.

The poor girl set off along the bank of the river, and, when she got near the wood, she sat down and began to sob and weep, and kept saying to herself: "Alas! where are you, my dear brothers? Are you dead or alive? Why does Bija yet live in spite of the insults of her sisters-in-law?"

It so happened that her brothers were just then returning home in a boat along the coast of the river, and, seeing their beloved sister Bija, they landed on the bank and enquired the reason of her presence there. She hastily dried her eyes, and, with the wonderful presence of mind of her sex, invented a story on the spur of the moment to account for it: "My sisters-in-law," said she, "are suffering from a kind of eye disease, so they have sent me here for a little of the milk from the Akanda plant."

The brothers immediately got together enough of it

[1] Asclepias gigantica.

in a cup made out of a leaf, and, taking their sister with them, hurried home.

As soon as their wives saw their husbands entering the house with Bija in their company, they trembled from head to foot, not knowing what was in store for them for all their harsh treatment of their sister.

" Are you suffering from an eye disease ? " said they to their wives. " Bija has been telling us that you sent her to fetch the milk of the Akanda plant, and so we have brought it to you."

The wives now felt more comfortable in their minds, for evidently Bija had not complained to her brothers about them. However, in order to keep up the pretence, they began to rub their eyes until they were red, and, lest their husbands should think they were shamming illness, they said : " Yes, we have nearly wept our eyes out for you, dear husbands, and that is the cause of our eye disease."

Saying this, they put a few drops of the Akanda milk into their eyes, and lo ! they became blind. They were afterwards taken away by their respective parents for treatment, but, having become permanently blind, they decided to stay with them for better care, and Bija and her brothers lived happily together as they had done before the wicked women came on the scene.

A NOSE FOR A NOSE.

ONCE upon a time there lived a certain miserly couple, and great misers they were. They used to keep but one servant between them, often starving him, and even cheating him out of his wages into the bargain. Before engaging one, they would say to him: "If thou leavest our service on any account thou shalt give thy nose to us; on the other hand, if we ever dismiss thee, thou shalt have our noses."

On these terms many a servant had served the couple, and, after having been starved and ill-treated, had at last wriggled himself out of the contract at the expense of his nose.

One day they took a boy into their service on the usual terms. They used to make him do all the drudgery of the household for them, but in return for all the work they got out of him he was put on short rations. "If the stomach is full, the back can bear," said the boy to himself, and, after a few days of semi-starvation and over-work, he too bought his freedom with his nose.

The boy went home empty-handed and noseless, and his younger brother, seeing his comic appearance, enquired how it all happened. He told him how his wicked employers had cunningly introduced the nose penalty into his contract of service, and then, by starving and over-working him, had made him break it, and so forfeit his nose.

The younger brother went straight off to the misers, determined to teach them a lesson, and offered to serve them on the same terms as his elder brother.

"Agreed," said the misers, with a mischievous twinkle in their eyes as they looked at each other, and the younger brother too was ill-fed and hard-worked "from early morn till dewy eve."

The boy, however, thought out a scheme of revenge in silence. When the couple had occasion to go out, the boy would steal into the pantry and help himself to all the bread, butter, and cakes.

In this way he had a nice time of it, while the misers began to fret and fume over his doings, but to no purpose. Of course, they could not dismiss him, or else they would have had to forfeit their own noses to him.

The troubles of the couple had now just begun. One day the boy was told to fetch some mutton for them, but, instead of buying it in the market, he had all their sheep slaughtered, and brought their mutton before them.

They flew into a rage and took the boy severely to task for it. They had not, they protested, told the boy to get their sheep slaughtered for the mutton.

The boy, however, with mock humility, said to them: "I am so sorry I misunderstood the order. You did not tell me to buy the mutton from the market. I thought you wanted *any* mutton, and here it is."

Of course, however much they wished to dismiss him then and there, they could not, and so they put the best face they could upon it.

On another occasion, when their only child was crying, the boy was told to keep it quiet. He gripped its throat so hard that it was strangled to death, and remained as quiet as the grave.

The miserly couple, now overwhelmed with grief at the death of their only child, did not know what to do to get rid of the troublesome boy. They feared their lives were not safe while he lived with them, so they planned to run away from the house temporarily, hoping he would in the meantime depart to his home.

After this decision, they buried all their valuables in divers secret places, and put some refreshments and a few other things, for use on the way, into a wooden trunk.

The boy, getting wind of their intention, squeezed himself somehow into the trunk, and lay in hiding there.

At dead of night the master of the house, with his wife, prepared to go off to the wife's home, and, lifting the trunk on to his shoulders, started off. The boy enjoyed the ride on the shoulders of his master, which felt as if he were being carried in a sedan chair, and ate up everything eatable he found inside the trunk.

After the two misers had gone a good way, they became tired and ravenously hungry with the long tramp, so they prepared to rest and refresh themselves. The trunk was put down on the ground near a well, and the lid lifted up, when lo! out leapt the boy from within it and almost perched on their heads. They screamed out as if he were a ghost let loose from hell, but, when they found it was the mischievous boy whom they wanted to avoid, they did not know whether to laugh or to weep. The boy stepped forth in front of them, and, folding his hands with mock humility, thus said to them: "Oh, my kind master and my kind mistress! how cruel of you to have intended to go away without me! I, on my part, cannot bear to be separated from you, so devoted a servant I am; and so, fearing to be left behind, I lay down in the trunk, making room for myself by putting all the sweets and cakes inside me."

If there was no food left to satisfy their hunger, there was, at any rate, plenty of water in the well to quench their thirst, and the boy, with pretended devotion, drew as much water for them as they could drink.

The husband and wife now determined to do away with the boy, and so they made three beds at some little distance from one another, the one nearest to the well being meant for their intended victim.

The boy, suspecting foul play, watched his master and mistress, and, when they had fallen into a deep slumber, got up on tip-toe, and, lying down between the two, pretended to snore the snore of the just.

Towards the darkest hour of dawn, his master got up, and, mistaking his wife for the boy, rolled her, blanket and all, down the well. As she fell with a splash, up sprang the boy, and his master, grieved and horrified, found out his mistake too late. Of course, he dared not tell him he had intended to throw him into the well, and not his wife, and so he attributed her fall to accident.

Instead of going back to an empty home, he continued his journey in order to inform his wife's parents of the mishap.

The boy, protesting devotion, persisted in accompanying him. At one moment he thought of ridding himself of his servant by giving up his nose, but at the next the idea of a noseless son-in-law appearing before his wife's family, and exciting laughter and amusement, instead of commiseration, among them, made him resign himself to his fate.

When they were nearing their destination, the boy ran ahead of his master and told this story to his master's father-in-law: "Sir," said the boy, addressing him, "thy son-in-law has suddenly gone raving mad. He is coming over here alone, leaving his wife behind at home; so thy daughter has sent me ahead to advise thee to put a few leeches on to his neck to let off some of his blood."

The boy then ran back to his master and told him he had just been to his father-in-law, like a dutiful servant, and informed him of his coming, so as to prepare him for his reception beforehand.

No sooner had the son-in-law arrived at his father-in-law's house than he was pounced upon by two stalwart fellows, like grim messengers of death, and found himself in their firm grip. Before he could make an attempt to speak, they had applied a number of leeches to the back of his neck to draw off the blood, the boy standing a little on one side enjoying the fun. As soon as their eyes met, his master cried out, maddened by the pain: "Come and take my nose, and begone, thou rascal!"

Of course, no lingering doubt was now left in the minds of the spectators as to his insanity, and the boy ran up to him, and, snipping off his nose, took to his heels.

Soon after, the miser's wife, rescued by a passer-by, arrived at her father's house, with cuts and bruises all over her face, and narrated all their woes to her parents.

Then her family saw how they had been imposed upon, and, cursing the mischievous boy from the bottom of their hearts, immediately took off the leeches.

The boy carried off his master's nose triumphantly, and put it on the stump of his brother's nose.

Thus had he revenged himself and exacted a nose for a nose.

THE JACKAL THE COMPLAINANT, THE GOAT THE ACCUSED, AND THE WOLF THE JUDGE.

ONCE upon a time a greedy jackal asked a bearded she-goat to take a lease of land and cultivate it in partnership with him.

The goat went straight off to a rack-renting landlord, (for all landlords are rack-renters,) and applied for a plot of land.

"Thou art but a goat," said the landlord, "and goats eat everything. They do not possess wits enough in proportion to their beards. Thou art sure to eat up thy crop, and wilt have nothing to pay my rent with. Begone!"

The goat went back to the jackal and told him of what had passed between the landlord and herself.

The jackal then took the goat to the landlord and offered to stand security for the rent, if he cared to let his land to the goat.

"Agreed," said the landlord, and away went the partners, rejoicing.

The rent fixed, they had yet to settle what should be grown on the land. The goat preferred cotton, which is of rather slow growth, while the jackal voted for melons, which were, of course, to his liking. However, in the true spirit of business, a compromise was arrived at, each meeting the other half-way. They grew half cotton and half melons.

Now they had to settle between themselves the hours of watch. In the end the goat agreed to guard the field by day, the jackal by night.

Soon there was a good crop of melons of all sizes, and the jackal began to lick his mouth as they ripened.

One night, during his watch, the jackal invited all his howling fraternity to a feast of melons, and all the melons disappeared.

The next day, when the goat's turn came to watch the field, she discovered the theft and immediately went and informed the jackal of their loss.

"Thou hast robbed me of my share of the melons," said the jackal angrily. "I saw them all right before I left the field. O greedy goat, thou must have eaten them thyself. I shall take thee before a judge."

The goat protested her innocence, wagging her beard to and fro solemnly.

The jackal then went away and appointed a wolf, as judge and umpire, to decide the quarrel, and at midnight he called for the goat and took her away before him.

The goat had reared up two orphan pups, and they, now full-grown, seeing their foster-mother go away with the jackal in the depth of the night, suspected something wrong and followed secretly.

Arrived at the den of the wolf, the jackal called out to him, and out came his honour in the peaceful robes of a judge, licking his mouth as he looked on the plump goat trembling in fear before him.

The jackal opened the case against the goat, and, by the time he had formulated his charges against her, day was breaking, and the wolf, at a pre-arranged sign from the jackal, sprang upon the prisoner. But at the same moment her two canine foster-children, who had followed her at a distance and had been watching the scene from behind a bush, sprang at his throat. The wolf cried out with pain to the jackal for help, but the latter said mockingly : " Why, art not thou the judge ? Punish thy assailants thyself," and with that he sneaked away with his tail between his legs, but not before one of the dogs had snapped off his nose.

After the victory, the dogs escorted their foster-mother safely home, leaving the wolf stretched at full length on the ground.

As for the jackal, he was made to pay the rent for the goat, and thus was punished for his roguery.

THE RIDDLE OF THE PUPPETS.

ONCE upon a time there was a certain King who had the curious habit of discussing affairs of State with his ministers in the most secluded portions of his private park, which was well laid out with shady trees and ornamented with artificial fountains.

One mid-day, the King, as was his wont, repaired thither with his Prime Minister, to hold a secret consultation. After they had finished their conversation, they went and sat down by a fountain, looking at the scenery all around them, when suddenly the King glanced up, and caught sight of a ripe mango on a branch just above his head. So tempting did it look, that the King asked his minister to pluck it for him, but he was not able to reach it.

"O Prince!" said the minister, after one or two vain efforts to get the fruit, "it is too high for me, and I am too old to climb up trees."

"There is no need to climb," replied the King with a smile. "Just get on to my shoulders and get it from there."

"I dare not presume so far," protested the minister, as he stood with hands folded. "Do thou rather, O Prince, mount upon my shoulders and bring it down."

"You are too old to bear my weight," said the King.

"Climb on my shoulders without any more fuss, sir. If you have any scruples, I, as your King, order you, as my subject, to do it."

After this, further parleys were useless.

"I am between the devil and the deep sea," thought the minister, as he prepared to do the King's bidding. So placing his feet, one on either shoulder of the King, he pulled the mango.

The King ate the fruit with great relish, as you may well imagine, after such mighty trouble, and then rose and returned to the palace with his minister.

The mango incident did not, however, pass unnoticed by other eyes than those of the King and his minister. While the latter stood on the shoulders of his royal master in the act of plucking the fruit, a saffron-robed mendicant happened to walk into the park unobserved, and witnessed the scene with a flutter of the heart. He immediately followed the King to the palace and prayed for an audience, which was granted after some delay.

"O Prince," said the mendicant, when he was ushered into his presence, "I crave thy royal pardon."

"What! My pardon?" exclaimed the King. "Why, hast thou committed any murder in my realm?"

"I have not," replied the mendicant, "nor do I ever intend to, yet I do feel I ought to have thy pardon."

"Then explain, thou silly man, why thou askest my pardon," cried the King, amazed beyond measure.

"There may be a cause or there may not," persisted the mendicant, "but still, all the same, I beg, O Prince, thy pardon."

"Very well," said the King, "thou art pardoned," but the mendicant, not yet fully satisfied, prayed him to put his pardon in writing under his hand and seal.

This was done, and the mendicant departed happily with the proof of his innocence, which he who ran might read.

Time flew on, and the King, for some reason or other, became offended with his Prime Minister and ordered him to be put to death—as was the practice of primitive days—with all his tribe, so that none might be left alive to avenge his death, or carry on a blood-feud from generation to generation. Among the relations of the condemned minister, the mendicant happened to be one, and so was led along with the others to the place of execution. When, however, it came to his turn to be executed, he held out the royal pardon, which he had carefully preserved all these long years, and the executioner, not knowing what to do, took him straight before the King.

The King, surprised to see the mendicant again, enquired what was the matter, and the latter, producing the pardon from the folds of his turban and showing it to the King, asked him in a tone of pious indignation why he had ordered his execution in violation of his plighted word.

The King ordered him to be released at once, and, taking him by the hand, retired into his private room with him. Before the King had recovered from his surprise and opened his lips, the mendicant thus began:

"O Prince! did not this 'silly man,' as thou wert pleased to call me, act wisely in having secured thy royal pardon in black and white? I once happened to take shelter against the heat of the sun in thy park, not knowing that thou wert alone with thy minister, and what should I see but thy servant, the minister, plant his feet on thy royal shoulders in order to pluck a mango! I was at once put in mind of the saying, 'Familiarity breeds contempt,' and the familiarity which began in the park then has now ended disastrously for him and his kith and kin. I was one of the latter, and, anticipating what has happened to-day, had taken care to ask thee for a written pardon in advance."

The King, admiring his uncommon intelligence and foresight, appointed him then and there his Prime Minister in place of his executed kinsman.

The executions over, the only surviving son of the late minister, who had escaped death by flight, sought and obtained an asylum with a protégé of his father's—the chief tailor to the King—and no more was thought of him. He was taught and was quick to learn sewing, besides ornamental work in gold and silver, and became generally useful to his protector.

As time went on, the King sent for his chief tailor, and, making over to him an ancient but valuable royal robe, ordered it to be wrought in gold. Now it so happened that this very youth undertook to do it himself, and began to work on it day and night without rest. As luck would have it, the King, who was in the habit of going about in disguise at night-time, to see with his own eyes how his subjects fared under his rule, passed by the house of his tailor one evening, and, seeing a light burning through an open window, peeped in. What was his indignation when he saw a youth sleeping with that very robe of his under his head for a pillow! He flew into a rage, and had the culprit arrested and brought before him for punishment.

"I suppose thou helpest thy master, my chief tailor, in his work," snapped the King, with thunder in his voice and lightning in his eyes. "How durst thou sleep with my royal robe beneath thy head? I will have thee beheaded."

"O Prince," replied the youth, meekly, "I put thy robe under my head for want of a better place to keep it."

"What?" cried the King angrily, "has thy master no trunk or wooden case in his house?"

"There are plenty of both in the house of my master," said the boy coolly.

"Then why didst thou not put it in one of them, instead of under thy head?" thundered out the King. "Thou deservest death."

"I have none to call my own in this wide, wide world," replied the youth with tears in his eyes, "and death has no longer any terrors for me. 'Strike, but hear' is my only prayer."

"Very well, say thy say," said the King, somewhat mollified.

"I put thy robe under my head, O Prince," he thus began, "because the head is the king of the body, and there could be no better place for a King's robe, I reflected, than under the head."

The King was pleased with his ingenious excuse and sent him away with a handsome reward for his cleverness.

Troubles, it has been said, never come alone, and, in the course of time, misfortunes crowded on the King. It so happened that a neighbouring monarch, instead of holding the usual *Swayamvara* (that is, a maiden's own choice of a husband from amongst assembled Princes) for his daughter, hit upon an ingenious device to discover the cleverest amongst the suitors for her hand. His plan was to send round to each Prince two puppets, apparently exactly similar in every respect. To the Prince who was able to decide which of the puppets was the better one he promised the hand of his daughter, and half his kingdom for dower.

Every other Prince had tried and failed, when it came to the turn of the King whose council chamber was his park. He too tried and failed, and the tailor boy, as the son of the late minister had come to be generally known, hearing of his failure, offered to solve the riddle of the puppets, which were accordingly made over to him.

The youth then took them with him into a lonely room and examined them carefully, when like a flash an idea struck him. He took up one puppet and dropped a needle into each of its ears, and found that the needles went in at the ears and out at the mouth. He applied the same test to the other puppet, but with a different result, as the needles, instead of going in at the ears and out at the mouth, remained inside.

In this way the riddle was solved, and the tailor boy returned the puppets to the King, pointing out which was the better one, without, however, giving his reason for the choice. The King at once sent back the puppets to their royal owner, saying which was the better one and demanding the hand of his daughter in accordance with the compact. The father of the Princess at once came and demanded of him his reasons for choosing the better puppet.

The King was now in a difficulty, and, sending for the tailor boy, asked him his reason for preferring one puppet to the other, but the youth refused to speak. He was then thrown into jail and threatened with all sorts of pains and penalties for his obstinacy, but he still refused to yield up his secret. The King, to save his face, asked for time in which to give his answer, under the pretext of formulating his reasons fully, for all is fair in love and war, they say; but in the meantime the other Prince found out who had solved the riddle, and the tailor boy was brought out of jail and questioned as to the reason of his choice of puppets.

"O Prince," said the youth, "I dropped needles into the ears of each of the puppets. In the case of one puppet the needles went in at the ears and out at the mouth, but in the case of the other they remained inside. The latter was, of course, the better puppet, as it conveyed the moral of 'silence is golden.'"

The logic was flawless, and both the Princes wondered how a mere tailor boy could carry such a clever head on his shoulders; but, on the latter explaining matters by telling them who he was—the son of no less a being than a Prime Minister—and his identity having been thoroughly established, he was at last rewarded in return for all the troubles he had undergone with the hand of the Princess and half a kingdom into the bargain. The two lived long and happily, and ruled their people well and wisely.

THE BRIDE OF THE SWORD.

ONCE upon a time a certain King had a harem of seven Queens, each the daughter of a King as great as himself, but by none of them had he been blessed with an heir. He prayed and sacrificed at many a shrine and many an altar, and at last the gods, thus propitiated, made him the proud father of seven Princes. They were brought up tenderly, and in time became the most accomplished of Princes. As they grew up into manhood, the King began to entertain thoughts of their marriage, and dreamt of grand-children playing at his knees, and so proclaimed, far and near, that royal brides were being sought for the Princes. Now it so happened that another King, whose State lay at some distance, had a family of seven beautiful daughters, and he, hearing of the proclamation, offered to give one in marriage to each of the seven Princes.

The offer was received with welcome relief, and there were great rejoicings throughout both the kingdoms at the approaching seven-fold wedding.

The six elder Princes and various ministers, each in order of rank and position, accompanied by the King at their head, started in gorgeous procession for the country of the brides, only the youngest remaining behind, at his own request, to look after the State in the absence of his father, and sending as proxy one of his jewelled swords.

Now it happened that there were two roads by which the country where dwelt the Princesses could be reached; one which took a long, tedious twelvemonths to traverse, and the other, which, though only a matter of twelve weeks' journey, was beset with peculiar perils. The King, however, did not dare to risk the lives of his dearly-loved sons, and ordered the procession to go by the safer though longer route. As the party went on, they made it a practice, whenever they halted, to cut details of the road on the tree-trunks, so as to facilitate their future journeys to and fro.

At the end of a twelvemonth, the travellers at last reached their destination, amidst demonstrations of popular joy, and the seven Princes were duly married, on one and the same day, to the seven charming Princesses—the youngest by his proxy, the sword.

After the wedding feasts were over, and the Princes and their party thoroughly refreshed, they started back for their country with their brides, each pair borne in a separate palanquin, one behind the other in order of their ages; and, as the number of their retainers was swollen by members of the brides' party, the King ventured to order the procession to take the shorter route. This they did, and followed the same practice as along the longer road, of cutting on the bark of trees particulars of the road they had passed through. In this way they went on and on without any misadventure, until one evening they came to a part of the road where a wicked magician lived; and, just as the party had turned a corner, they espied him striding towards them. There was no time to turn back and flee, far less to cut a warning on a tree, for the magician stood before them in a trice and muttered an incantation, when lo and behold! all the members of the party turned to marble as they stood, palanquins, horses, and all!

After having wrought the transformation, the magician went back to his castle, feeling as sure of his booty as if it were under lock and key.

One, however, out of the numerous company had escaped the magic spell. The last palanquin, which contained the youngest Princess, wedded by proxy to the sword, had luckily been hidden by the bend in the road, and so escaped the sight of the magician. The bearers, who had foolishly put down the palanquin and run ahead to see what was stopping the procession, had shared the fate of the others and been turned into stone. The Princess, creeping out of her palanquin, witnessed the tragedy, and was at her wits' end how to save herself from the clutches of the magician.

As darkness thickened around her, wolves and jackals began to set up their hideous cries in the distance, and the frightened Princess, seeing a light burning not far from the road, took up the wedded sword and ran straight towards it. She ran and ran until she found herself, trembling and gasping for breath, in front of a fine mansion, the door of which was closed.

She knocked hard at the door and kept saying: "Whoever lives in this house, open the door to a distressed Princess. I call thee father if thou art a male. I call thee mother if thou art a female."

Suddenly the door flew open, and whom should she see but an ugly being who took her by the hand and led her inside, slamming the door after him! Her guide proved to be none other than the wicked magician—she had indeed walked into a lion's den unawares.

"Know me, O Princess, to be the magician-robber of this road," said he. "No living thing ever comes alive to my castle, but thy life will I spare because thou hast called me father."

The Princess, grateful for having her life spared, thanked him for the asylum which he offered her, and began to live at his castle

A long time had gone by since the wedding procession had departed, and the youngest Prince, who had remained behind, wisely, as the event showed, to look after the kingdom while his father was abroad, became very anxious. At last, despairing of their return, he placed the kingdom in charge of one of his trusted ministers and left home alone in disguise, in search of his long-absent father and brothers. In his eagerness to see them, he started by the shorter route and journeyed on until he came to the most perilous part of the road. Arrived there, he looked around and was surprised to see, close to him, the whole wedding party, including his father and six brothers, as if they were halting there. He ran up to where his father stood and embraced him, but, horror of horrors! he felt as if he had embraced a statue, as indeed he had done. He felt sure that some potent magician had been at work, and how the spell could be broken now engrossed his mind.

Worn out by the journey, and overcome by hunger and thirst, he began to search for wild fruit and water, and, seeing a mansion hard by, ran towards it. Arrived at the door, he knocked at it, and kept saying as he knocked: "Whocver lives in this house, open the door to a distressed Prince. I call thee brother if thou art a male. I call thee sister if thou art a female."

This form of address would appear to have been a necessary precaution in days of yore, when the only tie held sacred was the tie of kinship. No one would think of slaying one claiming kinship with him, lest the blood of the slain should be on the head of the slayer.

No sooner had he uttered the words than the door flew open, and a charming Princess let him in with a graceful bow, and closed the door after her.

The Princess was surprised to behold such a handsome youth, and no less surprised was the Prince to find a beautiful and lonely maiden shut up in the castle. They soon told each other of all their woes and who they were, and how great was their astonishment when the Princess beheld in the Prince her own husband, married to her by proxy, and the Prince beheld in the Princess his own bride, wedded to his sword! But alas! they were henceforth to be to each other no more than brother and sister. In what an ill-starred moment did the Prince say as he knocked at the door: "Whoever lives in this house, open the door to a distressed Prince. I call thee brother if thou art a male. I call thee *sister* if thou art a female!"

"A deed," said the philosophers of ancient India, "cannot die." As thou sowest, so shalt thou reap.

The Prince and Princess bowed to their fate and promised to be brother and sister to each other.

Needless to say, as they were in the castle of the wicked magician, there was but little time to indulge in regrets; indeed, whilst they were speaking, the magician was already at the door, knocking for admission.

Now it happened that the Princess had learnt just a little magic under the magician's roof, and, as soon as she heard him knocking at the door, she immediately turned the Prince into a fly, and ran down and opened the door. Every day, when the magician went out, she would restore the Prince to his own form, and she would turn him into a fly again when the magician returned. Thus their days passed away, not, however, without a great yearning for their own home. Filled with thoughts of escape, the Prince asked the Princess to coax and cajole the magician into telling her the secret of how to restore to flesh and blood their kinsfolk who had been turned to marble by his spell. The Princess did as she was bid.

"O father," she began, when one evening she sat chatting with the magician, "thou hast not taught thy daughter all the magic thou knowest. Couldst thou restore to life the marble statues outside the castle?"

"Oh, yes, of course, and that by a very simple process," replied the magician, thoughtlessly. "There is a well of ambrosia in this castle, and all one need do is to sprinkle a few drops of it over the marble figures, and in an instant these will come to life and move again."

The Princess treasured up the secret in her heart, and, when the magician was away, imparted it to the Prince. They were delighted at the success of their diplomacy, but, so long as the magician lived, they dared not make use of their knowledge to undo the magic. So their next plan was to worm out of the magician the secret of what thing it was on which his life depended.

And so again, one evening, the Princess set her little trap for the unwary magician. As they sat chatting, the Princess let fall one or two tears on his feet. He started up.

"What is the matter with thee, my daughter?" asked the magician. "What aileth thee?"

The Princess, not slow to take the tide at the flood, began to lay her snares thus: "O father," said she, "what torments me is the fear of what would happen to me if I should lose thee?"

"Oh, is that what aileth thee, my daughter?" said the magician, now altogether thrown off his guard by her tears. "Let thy mind be set at rest once and for all. A magician wears a charmed life, and cannot die until the charm be undone."

"In what thing, may I know, O father, does the charm of thy life lie, if thou dost not care to hide it from thy beloved daughter?" queried the daughter, coaxingly.

"Far away on an island," said the magician, "there is a tree. On the tree there hangs a cage. In the cage there is a bird. In the bird there is an egg, and in the egg lies the charm of my life. If the egg be broken in twain, my life will depart. The task is beyond all mortal power, so do not fret, my dear daughter."

The Princess now dried her eyes and turned the conversation to happier themes.

After the magician had gone out as usual, the Princess told the Prince how she had again been successful, and in what thing lay the magician's life.

The Prince now took leave of the Princess. "O Princess," said he as he kissed her good-bye, "I am starting for that far-away island in search of the life-bird of the magician. If I succeed in my adventure, I shall come back to thee, but should I fail, then this may be my last adieu."

At midnight, when the magician was snoring, the Princess restored the Prince to his form and let him out of the castle, sorrowfully.

He journeyed on and on until, just before dawn, he lay down beneath a way-side tree for a snatch of sleep, with his head upon his shield and his sword in his hand. Before he had been asleep many moments, he heard a hissing sound, and at once sprang to his feet with the sword in his hand, to behold a huge snake crawling up the tree. He instantly cut it in pieces with his sword, and, gathering these up under the shield, lay down to sleep again as if nothing had happened. Now it so chanced that a pair of enormous eagles had reared their young ones in a nest on that very tree, and had been missing some one or other of their numerous brood for some time. The parent birds, which had left the nest just before, to search for food for their young ones, returned soon after, only to find the young birds almost dead with fright. They saw the Prince lying full length upon the ground just beneath the tree, and at once jumped to the conclusion that he must have done something to frighten the young ones. They would have at once attacked him with their beaks and claws, had not the young ones themselves assured them that, so far from attempting to do them any harm, he had actually saved them from a monstrous serpent, and that, if they would only lift the shield and peep under it, they would find who was their real enemy. The parent birds flew down quickly and lifted up the shield with their beaks, when they were horrified to see a huge snake chopped into a thousand pieces under it. They at once knew who had been molesting their young ones so long, and, in gratitude for what the Prince had done, the birds stood, one on each side, shading him with their wings, and kept guard over him.

When the Prince awoke, he was surprised to see the birds watching over him. They told him how grateful they felt to him for having destroyed their common enemy, and asked him how they could best show their gratitude.

"Oh, do not talk of gratitude," said the Prince, "you are but birds, and birds can be of little use to me in my adventure. However," he thought to himself, "just as a thief is set to catch a thief, so may a bird be set to catch a bird." He told them whither he was bound, and with what object, and the birds, asking him to wait where he was until they returned, flew away with lightning speed to the island, and, seizing the cage with the bird in it, flew back to the Prince.

The magician happened to be away at the time, but, having had a presentiment of his coming doom, hastened with all speed to save his life-bird. As soon as the Prince saw him coming towards him at full speed, he wrenched off one of the bird's legs, and the magician thereupon instantly lost one leg. Still he kept hobbling along upon the other until the Prince broke the bird's remaining leg, and the magician now began to crawl upon his hands. Before he could come near enough to seize the bird, however, the Prince had killed it and broken open the egg, when lo! the magician rolled over upon the ground, dead, shrieking with his last breath: "This is thy work, O my daughter. Ingratitude, O woman, is thy name!"

The birds now carried the Prince to the Princess, and when he told her how he had wrought the death of the magician, she received the news with mingled feelings of joy and sorrow—joy at the prospect of soon seeing her beloved sisters alive again, and sorrow because she had been the indirect cause of the death of one she had lived with so long. The Prince and Princess then went to the well of ambrosia, and, carrying a bowl filled with it to the marble statues, sprinkled it over them, and lo! the whole party at once began to move as if they had just been awakened from their sleep! The youngest Prince now embraced his father and his brothers in turn, and told them how he had found them turned to marble, and how by the help of birds he had succeeded in killing the magician, and finally with ambrosia restored them to life.

The party now resumed their journey amidst great rejoicing. They at last reached home and were received with joy, as one might expect after such a long absence.

Only the youngest Princess was unhappy, because she was now no more than a sister to her husband. Her real husband henceforth was the sword; for had she not been married to it with the recitation of sacred verses? She now began to lavish all her affections upon it. She would talk to it and fondle it, and could not suffer it to be out of her sight even for a moment. It was her constant companion, sleeping or waking, in weal or woe.

The youngest Prince naturally resented the favour shown to his sword instead of to him, and, in a fit of jealousy, sought to snatch it away from her; but at this she clasped it all the more firmly, and her heart, already well-nigh broken, was pierced through and through. With the sword upon her bosom, she lay dead!

THE FOOLISH VOW.

ONCE upon a time a foolish young Prince made a silly vow, which was to cost him dear. "Whoever shall wed me," he used to say to himself and his companions, chuckling over the idea, "must submit to be beaten five times with a shoe, the first thing every morning. What fun I shall have! I delight to see Beauty in tears."

Of course, as might have been expected, no sensible girl cared to marry him, albeit he was a Prince, on such a humiliating condition; for a girl would sooner choose love in a cottage than love in a palace with the dreadful prospect of a daily shoe-beating. However, there are girls *and* girls, and it so happened that a young Princess, attracted by the novelty of the vow, chose him for her husband, notwithstanding the protests of her parents and the counsels of her friends.

The very first morning after the wedding, the Prince woke his sleeping bride up and asked her to prepare herself for her "honeymoon," as he ironically termed the chastisement he had in store for her. The Princess sat up on the edge of her bed and began to rub her eyes.

"Oh, my dear husband," she pleaded with bewitching tongue and eye, "put it off for a few days. What a shame to welcome me with a shoe-beating ere my feet are well across thy threshold! Canst thou not reserve this, thy loving reception of thy bride, for some other day? I assure thee, thou mayst then exact all thine arrears of beating with compound interest. I do not like to have my beating in driblets."

After a few days of married life, which nothing seemed to mar, the Princess returned to her parents, in order to give her husband an opportunity to repent of his vow during her absence. The Prince had fallen head over ears in love with the Princess, and so, before she had been long with her parents, he sent for her. When she returned to him, he again asked her if she was ready to receive the postponed punishment in fulfilment of his vow.

"Oh, my dear husband," said she, "how darest thou threaten me with a beating, as if I were thy slave? During infancy a woman is maintained by her father, during marriage by her husband, and during widowhood by her sons. A *vartâ* [1] or husband is, therefore, 'one who supports his wife,' but, although thou callest thyself my husband, thou art but my husband in name, for it is not thou that maintainest me, but thy father, the King. Go abroad and earn for thyself the wherewithal to maintain thy wife, and then carry out thy vow if thou carest to. A husband unable to support his wife has no right to exercise his power over her."

Stung to the quick by these taunts, the Prince had a ship fitted out with merchandise by his father, and sailed away in the hope of returning home with enough money of his own to entitle him to the name of husband, and so confer the right to exercise his power over

[1] The Sanskrit word for husband—*vartâ*—is derived from the root *vri*, "to support."

his wife. As a precaution, he took care to carry with him a carrier-pigeon, so as to be able to send a message home to his father in case of need.

After some days at sea, the ship entered a harbour which was infested by swindlers. One of these, who was possessed of but one leg, jumped on board and thus addressed the Prince: "I took, O Prince, a thousand gold coins from thy grandfather on a mortgage of one of my legs a long, long time ago. Be pleased, therefore, to take his money and return me my leg."

The Prince, taken aback by such a claim, cried out: "I never saw any leg with my grandfather. Surely thou must be mistaken!"

"Do not try to deceive me, O Prince," replied the swindler. "Thou must return my leg, or else I will not leave thy ship."

The Prince, not knowing how to get rid of his troublesome visitor, and at the same time deeming it the pious duty of a grandson to discharge the obligations of his ancestor, paid him double the value of his leg, and bade him begone.

The ship then weighed anchor and set sail for another port, where, too, no sooner had the ship arrived than another swindler, a man with one eye, ran on board, and, seeking out the Prince, thus said to him: "O Prince! thy grandfather holds one of my eyes by way of mortgage for a thousand gold coins. Be pleased to take his money and return my eye."

"I know of no such transaction," replied the Prince, amazed. "Surely, if any eye had been mortgaged with my grandfather, I would have seen it. Thou art mistaken."

"Surely, O Prince," retorted the one-eyed swindler, "thou art trying to evade thy obligations to thy ancestor. Return my eye, or I will not budge an inch from where I am."

The Prince rid himself of him, too, by paying double the value of his eye.

Again the ship set sail and made for a third port, which, it was hoped, would be free from pests of this kind, and might give the Prince a chance to turn his goods into money; but the Fates ordained otherwise. A far more cunning impostor than the two whom the Prince had already encountered soon had him in her grip; for this time it was a woman.

Hardly had the ship entered the harbour when she came on board, and, claiming the Prince as her nephew, flung herself upon him, saying: "O my dear nephew, thou art welcome! Come and spend a day with me before thou goest away. Thou needest a little rest. Thy father and grandfather, whenever they happened to come to this port, always stopped with me for a day or two's rest."

The Prince, not suspecting anything wrong, accompanied her to her house, where he was sumptuously entertained by his pretended aunt.

At midnight, however, while the Prince was fast asleep, the old woman walked on tip-toe into his room, slipped a tiny little silver key into one of the pockets of his coat which hung on the wall, and then slunk back to her bed.

Next morning the Prince bade good-bye to his "aunt" and returned to his ship, but she soon followed him, crying "Thief! thief!"

The Prince, annoyed at the woman crying "Thief,

thief!" when no thief was in sight, asked her why she was making such an uproar for nothing.

"Thou art the thief, and hast abused my hospitality," cried out the old crone, "by stealing my silver key."

"Thou must be mad, my dear aunt," said the Prince. "If thou findest thy key anywhere on this ship, the ship itself with all its cargo shall be thine, but, if thou failest to find it, wilt thou be willing that all thy goods shall be mine?"

"Agreed," said the woman with a twinkle of mischief in her eyes. She now pretended to make a long and detailed search, throwing everything topsy-turvy, and, just when the Prince was congratulating himself on having the best of the bargain, she demanded that his person should be searched. Sure enough, the tiny silver key was found lying snugly in a pocket of his coat!

The Prince stood amazed, unable to deny the charge, and in the end had to hand over his ship and its cargo to the woman, in accordance with the pact.

The Prince having now lost all, wandered into the city and was in sore straits as to what to do. At last, tormented by hunger, he was compelled to become the slave of an oil-monger for the sake of food, raiment, and shelter. He worked at the oil-mill from morning till night, crushing out oil from seeds. He put down all his troubles to his not having carried out his matrimonial vow, and so, smarting under the pain and indignity of it all, wrote two notes, one to his wife, in which he said he was returning home laden with gold and silver, and warning her to be ready to receive her long-delayed beating, and the other to his father, informing him of his distress, and asking for speedy assistance.

These notes he tied, one to each leg of the pigeon he had brought with him, and sent it off. Away it flew with the message, and on its arrival home dropped exhausted in the very quarters of the Princess. She speedily caught the bird, took the notes off, and read them both, one by the light of the other. She at once guessed that her letter was a mere make-believe, while the letter to her father-in-law told the truth, and that her husband was indeed but a slave to an oil-merchant.

Determined to say nothing, she kept the contents of the notes to herself and went back to her parents. She then informed her father of the miserable plight of her husband, and, dressing herself up as a Prince, loaded a fast-sailing ship with merchandise and set sail in search of him.

At the first port she reached, the same one-legged impostor who had fleeced her husband boarded the ship and, addressing her, thus began : "O Prince, my leg is in mortgage with thy grandfather for a thousand gold pieces. Be pleased to take back his money and return my leg."

The Princess was, of course, too clever to be taken in and fleeced by such a rogue. She took the money coolly, and, determined to pay him back in his own coin, answered him thus : "Oh, yes, I think I have seen a lot of legs mortgaged by different people with my grandfather. I really do not know to whom each of them belongs, but I will find thine out. However, to make sure that I do not give thee the wrong one, I must have thine other leg cut off and weighed in the scales against the others, one by one. If the weight of this leg of thine exactly balances any other leg, that, surely, must be thine ;" and without more ado she ordered one of her armed men to seize the rascal and cut off his leg. The rogue, however, did not wait for him to approach, but hobbled away as fast as he could on his one leg.

After this adventure, the Princess ordered the ship to weigh anchor and make for the next port, and here, too, as soon as the ship came in, the one-eyed swindler leaped on board, and, spreading out a thousand gold coins before the Princess, cried out: "O Prince, I once borrowed a thousand gold coins of thy grandfather, and as security mortgaged one of my eyes to him. Take back his money and return my eye."

The Princess took the money and thus replied to the rogue: "Oh, yes, I have seen a lot of mortgaged eyes with my grandfather, but I do not know which is thine. Well, I must have thine other eye too, for it is only by weighing it in the scales against the other eyes, one by one, that I may know the one mortgaged by thee. If two eyes weigh the same, both must be thine;" and, saying that, she ordered one of her retainers to pluck out his other eye.

The rogue, finding himself caught in his own trap, did not wait to be seized, but jumped overboard and swam ashore.

The ship was soon under weigh again, and making for the port where lived the wicked woman who had robbed the Prince of all he had by her knavery. No sooner did the ship put into harbour than this same old crone came on board and thus introduced herself to the disguised Princess: "I am thy aunt, O my dear nephew. Thou art welcome to this port. Do come and rest with thy aunt for a day. Thy father and grandfather, whenever they came here, never refused my invitation."

The Princess well knew that she was no kinswoman of hers, yet, wishing to see what would come of it, she decided to accept the invitation and go with the woman to her house. She was as grandly entertained as her husband had been before, but, for all that, the Princess never once allowed herself to be put off her guard. So when, after the feast, the Princess went to bed, she kept awake, awaiting further developments; and lo! at midnight her self-styled aunt, thinking the Princess asleep, stole into her room, slipped a tiny silver key into a pocket of her coat, which hung in its place on the wall, and then disappeared as suddenly as an apparition.

After she was gone the Princess got up, went to her coat, took the key out of its pocket, and, dropping it into a water-jug which stood on a table near her bed, went back to sleep.

When the morning dawned, the Princess took leave of the woman and went back to her ship. Soon after her departure, however, the old beldame came running on board her ship, crying: "Thief, thief!" at the top of her voice.

"Thief? Thief? Where? Where?" cried the Princess, as she looked around her, startled.

"O my nephew! O my nephew!" said the woman, "thou art the thief. Thou hast abused the hospitality of thy aunt by carrying away her silver key."

"Thou must be a mad woman to charge thy nephew with the theft of thy key," replied the Princess mockingly.

"Well," retorted the woman, "if the key is found on thee, art thou willing to forfeit thy ship and all its cargo to me?"

"Agreed," replied the Princess, "provided that thou art prepared to lose all thou ownest to me, should it not be found on me."

Thus was the matter arranged, and a long search followed, but the key was not to be found. The Princess thereupon had the woman seized and her house searched, when, sure enough, the tiny little silver key was found lying at the bottom of her water-jug!

The woman had now the worst of the bargain, and the Princess recovered, without difficulty, her husband's ship with all its rich cargo, besides many valuables belonging to the woman herself, which were presumably the proceeds of a long series of crimes and frauds.

Emboldened by this success, she now went into the city to look for her husband, and soon came upon him working in the mill of his master, the oil-merchant. She sought the latter out and ransomed her husband, but took care to have a written agreement transferring him to herself.

Armed with this document, she set her husband free. He on his part, not knowing who his benefactor was, so cleverly had the Princess disguised herself, was profuse in his gratitude. Not doing things by halves, the Princess restored to him his ship and cargo, and both set out for home in their respective ships.

When they were nearing their country, the Princess took leave of the Prince with mutual protestation of friendship, and, pressed by the latter to accept something as a souvenir, asked for the ring he was wearing, which was at once given.

The Prince, on the other hand, sold her all his cargo and, with the money thus obtained, hoped to make it appear that he had prospered exceedingly on his travels, as his letter to the Princess had stated. And so the two parted.

The Princess returned to her parents some time before the Prince, for hers was the faster of the two ships, and, after throwing off her disguise and putting on a Princess's robe, went to her father-in-law's house to await her husband's coming. Of course, her father-in-law knew nothing of her adventures, nor had he any inkling of the distress his son, the Prince, had brought upon himself by his folly.

The Prince soon returned home, and, meeting his wife, smiling a sort of tell-tale smile, at the threshold, stiffened himself up and ordered her to be ready for the shoe-beating he had put off so long at her request; at the same time giving her to understand that he would have no more of her excuses now that he had brought home enough money to keep half-a-dozen wives in luxury and idleness.

"What?" exclaimed the Princess with pretended indignation. "Can a slave exercise any powers over his mistress? Thou art my slave." So saying, she held out before his bewildered eyes the deed by which the oil-merchant had transferred him to herself.

He still hesitated to believe her, even in the face of the writing, about which there could be no mistake; but when she told him, in detail, how the carrier-pigeon had arrived with his message of distress, and dropped exhausted almost in her lap; how she had sailed, disguised as a Prince, in a ship fitted out for her by her father, and braved winds and waves in search of him; how she had outwitted the one-legged and one-eyed swindlers, and even the wicked crone herself; and, finally, how she had come upon him working as a slave and ransomed him; and, further, produced the very ring he had given her as a parting gift; then, and then only, did all his lingering doubts vanish into thin air.

From that time forward the Prince and Princess lived together happily, and no word of a shoe-beating was ever mentioned.

THE PEARL GOOSE.

ONCE upon a time there lived in great poverty a man who had seen better days, with his wife, an exacting and heartless woman. He used to earn a miserable living by collecting fuel in the woods and selling it in the market.

One day, the man was not able to collect enough fire-wood for both consumption and sale, and so this virago of a wife gave him nothing to eat. So back he went, hungry, to the wood to collect more fuel, and, sitting down under a tree, began to sob and cry. Overhead on a branch there dwelt a gander and a goose, and these, seeing him weep, enquired the reason of his tears.

"You are but birds," sobbed out the poor man. "How could you possibly be of any help to me, even if I told you?"

"We are birds, to be sure," replied the goose, moved to pity, "but all the same I think I could help to relieve thy distress if thou wouldst tell me all about it."

He then took the bird into his confidence and told her how poverty was crushing the very life out of him, not forgetting to add a word about the treatment meted out to him by his wife at home.

"Women, like moths, are caught by gold," said the goose, as she threw down a couple of pearls towards him. "Take these home to thy wife and come to me daily for a pair of pearls so long as thou livest. I lay two pearls every day."

The poor man jumped for joy, and, thanking the goose, took the pearls home to his wife. Needless to say, she was overjoyed at this turn of luck, and took good care to wake up her husband every morning and send him to the goose for his allowance of two pearls a day.

They had now become prosperous, and in their prosperity they ceased to be grateful to their benefactor, and even sought to do her harm.

"My dear husband," said the wicked woman one day, as the man was going to the wood, "the pearl goose has been so kind to us that I should like thee to bring her to our house to-day. I want to give her a treat as a small return of her kindness."

Unsuspicious of her design, he went to the pearl goose and asked her to return home with him. The goose accepted his invitation and accompanied him to his house, but lo! no sooner had she arrived there than the wicked woman, with an evil smile on her face, rushed forward and catching hold of one of the bird's wings, said: "Art thou the pearl goose? Hast thou been making my husband come to thee and beg for pearls all this time? I will see to it that thou shalt trouble him no more, for I will cut thee open and get all the pearls out of thee at once, and thus save my husband the trouble of a daily visit to thee. I have never tasted a pearl goose, but I am sure thy flesh must taste sweet. We will make a feast of thee."

The pearl goose found herself caught in a pretty trap; the invitation was of course a feint.

The woman now began to drag the goose in through the door, but the bird spread out her wings against the door and so made her efforts useless. She called out to her husband to come and help her, so that between them they might force the bird through the door. Afraid of his wife, he caught hold of one wing while his wife held the other, and there thus began a long tug-of-war between the bird on one side and the wicked pair on the other, and a large crowd gathered to watch the contest.

The King of the land, who was going out to hunt, happened to pass by, and, seeing this cruel scene, rescued the bird from the hands of her oppressors. The pearl goose then complained to the King about the ingratitude of the couple, and, when he had heard everything, he ordered all the pearls which were found in the house to be surrendered to him by way of punishment; and so these ungrateful wretches lapsed back into their former poverty.

The King, for his part, congratulated himself upon having found this precious bird. He carried her home and took great care of her. After the day's cares and worries of State, he would pass his time pleasantly in talking with the pearl goose, for the goose was endowed with the gift of human speech and was a store-house of information in herself, having travelled far and wide.

The King, who was very fond of hunting, happened one day to be out with his hounds. The Queen, not liking the bird to be lonely, had her brought to her and began to amuse her.

"My dear pearl goose," said the Queen, addressing the bird, "thou must have flown all over the world. Hast thou ever seen a handsomer woman than thy mistress?"

The pearl goose made no answer. She repeated the question, and yet there was no answer. The Queen then ventured to put the question for the third time, when the bird at last broke her silence.

"There is a saying, O Queen, 'Speak the truth, but beware of uttering that which is unpleasant;' for one who tells an unpalatable truth shares in the odium which attaches to it."

"I do not want thee to flatter me with pleasing falsehoods," replied the Queen. "Tell me if thou hast ever seen a handsomer woman than I am."

"I had no mind to say anything likely to offend thee," said the pearl goose reluctantly, "but, since thou insistest on it, there is no help for it but to tell thee the truth. Thou boastest thyself to be a beauty without a peer in heaven or earth," continued the goose, "but thy face would appear ugly compared to a toe of the daughter of the King of the Singhal Island. She is the Pearl of the East!"

"What?" exclaimed the Queen in anger. "Thou comparest my face to a toe? Thou hast no eye for beauty." With that, she called a servant and bade him take the bird away and pluck her eyes out.

The servant obeyed his mistress, but, before he could leave the palace with the bird, he was caught at the gate by the porter and detained as a thief. He assured him, however, he was no thief, but was simply carrying out the orders of the Queen.

"Depend upon it," said the porter, when he was told the nature of the order, "this is no ordinary bird. The King is extremely fond of her, and so, if he misses her on his return, he may have thee hanged, drawn, and quartered."

At this the servant went away, frightened, with the precious bird, and instead of killing it he had the eyes of another goose gouged out, and these he brought to the Queen as proofs of his having carried out her order.

Some time after this, the King returned from hunting and went straight to his favourite bird, the pearl goose. Missing her from her accustomed place, he sent for all his servants and enquired what had become of the bird, but they were too frightened to tell him. The porter, however, told him how the Queen, in a fit of anger, had ordered the eyes of the pearl goose to be gouged out, and how he had warned the man to whom the cruel task was entrusted not to carry out her order. In the meantime this man, hearing of the return of the King, brought back the pearl goose and was rewarded for his pains.

The King next went into the chamber of the Queen and took her to task for having ordered the eyes of his favourite bird to be put out.

"O King," said the Queen, with tears in her eyes and darkening brows, "I have been grossly insulted by thy over-spoilt bird, the pearl goose. She dared to compare my face to a toe of the Pearl of the East, as she chose to call the daughter of the King of the Singhal Island. Could flesh and blood stand it? She had no eye for beauty, and that is why I ordered her stupid eyes to be scooped out of their sockets."

"O Queen, I find that thy order has not been carried out for fear of my anger. The pearl goose is unharmed. However, if she has told thee a lie, I will not only have her eyes plucked out but will have her put to a torturing death. I must see the Pearl of the East with my own eyes."

The Queen had not thought of this; it was, she feared, going to be a case of falling from the frying-pan into the fire for her.

The King immediately went back to the pearl goose and asked her to show him the Pearl of the East. The pearl goose warned him against possible dangers on the way, but the King turned a deaf ear to all her warnings. Reluctantly the bird took him up on her wings and flew away in the direction of the island where the Pearl of the East dwelt. At midnight, when the Princess was sleeping, the pearl goose put the King down at her bedroom window and waited outside. As the pearl goose had said, she was indeed a paragon of beauty and fully justified her name, for verily was she the Pearl of the East. The pearl goose had spoken the truth, the whole truth, and nothing but the truth, about her beauty, and the King straightway fell in love with her. But, fearing lest too abrupt a confession of love might defeat its object, he contented himself with exchanging rings with her, while she was asleep, before returning to his palace.

The following night, at his request, the pearl goose again took the King to the Singhal Island, and, leaving him at the same window, waited outside.

As on the previous night, the King again found the Princess asleep, and, exchanging his garland with hers, returned to his kingdom.

Next morning, when the Princess awoke, she was surprised to see a strange garland round her neck in place of her own, and she now for the first time noticed that her ring had been exchanged for another. She told her mother what had happened, and she in her turn told the King, who at once ordered special guards to be set all round the palace, and, as a special precaution against the escape of the unknown visitor, caused all the approaches to his daughter's room to be greased, so as to render more difficult any intruder's escape.

Next night the King, in blissful ignorance of these precautions, again arrived at the island, and, as he stepped on to the window, down he slipped and fell right upon the heads of the guards below. He was at once captured and straightway taken before the King of the island, who ordered him to be instantly executed.

The royal victim was then taken to the usual place of execution, which happened to be beneath an ancient tree, and on this tree the pearl goose, which had followed him on the wing overhead, had perched itself. The King asked for a few minutes in which to make his peace with his Maker before meeting his doom, and the guards granted him this not unnatural request. The King pretended to be absorbed in his prayers, whilst his captors sat chatting and smoking beneath the tree. Suddenly, at a sign from the pearl goose, he rose and clambered up the tree in the twinkling of an eye. Before the stupefied guards could attempt to catch him, the bird had lifted him on to her wings and flown away.

Nothing daunted, the King went again on the following night to the Singhal Island, but, profiting by the bitter experience of the night before, he had taken the precaution of rubbing some sticky substance on the soles of his feet. So, when the pearl goose dropped him as usual at the window of the Princess's bedroom, he did not, of course, slide down, but descended safely into the room and walked straight to the bed-side of the Princess. She had kept awake so as to see her lover, and as his handsome figure appeared she sat up on her bed, and forthwith fell in love with him at first sight!

"O Princess," began the King, "I have already married thee in accordance with the form of marriage—*Gandharva*—sanctioned by Manu, the law-giver, for members of the ruling caste; for have we not exchanged rings and garlands? I have now come to take thee, my bride, to my kingdom, but thou must not let thy father know of our marriage nor of my presence here, or he will surely kill both of us." There was, of course, no denying the marriage by exchange of rings and garlands, and the Princess, who had by now quite lost her heart to her royal spouse, set off with him to his kingdom without even so much as a good-bye to her parents.

And so the King brought the Pearl of the East to his palace after all, and, as the pearl goose had said, her toes far exceeded in beauty even the face of the boastful Queen. In time the Queen, as well as the pearl goose came to be neglected by the King in favour of his new favourite—the Pearl of the East.

Heart-broken, the one went back to her parents while the other, home-sick, flew back to her nest amidst the trees to meet her mate, from whom she had been so long absent.

The Pearl of the East thus began to rule the royal household with none to rival her in the King's affection.

THE UNGRATEFUL GOAT.

ONCE upon a time a greedy goat, while out grazing with his flock, strayed away into the depth of the forest. At nightfall the flock returned to its fold, leaving the silly goat to his fate.

As darkness came on, he stopped grazing and turned round to look for his companions, but to his horror he found no trace of them, while the howls of wolves and jackals in the distance made him realize his danger, but too late. In fear and trembling, he ran hither and thither in search of shelter, but, alas! none was to be found.

Whilst trying to find his way in the dark, he happened to come upon a lion's footprints, and, terrified at the sight, he crouched down and awaited his fate. Soon afterwards a pack of wolves came up, making the night hideous with their cries, but, before they could spring upon him and tear him to pieces, he gathered his wits together, and, with a bow, thus shouted out to them :

"Wolves, have you seen my master, the lion, returning?"

"The lion! The lion! What lion?" they cried out, all at once, at the same time leaping a dozen yards back and looking around, much frightened.

"I mean the king of this forest," said the goat calmly, having overcome his fears by supreme efforts. "He has just left me for a minute, asking me to wait for him at this spot," and in proof he pointed to the footmark he was squatting upon. To be sure, it was a footprint of a lion, and the wolves, believing the goat, went away sullenly to look for their prey elsewhere.

Next came a leopard, licking his lips as he beheld the plump goat before him, and, as he crouched down, cat-like, for a spring, the goat told him the same tale as he had told the wolves, and with such effect that Mr. Spots, too, went away disappointed.

Last of all came the lion, the king of the forest, and no sooner did the goat see him appear, than he embraced his foot-mark with his forehoofs and began to kiss it fervently, as if it were the god of his destiny. The lion, surprised at the strange behaviour of the goat, asked him what it was all about. "I belong, Sir Lion!" said the goat, whining, "to the flock of a prince. Misfortune has separated me from my companions, and, having found myself alone in this forest surrounded by horrid beasts of prey, I have taken refuge in the sanctuary of thy footmark. Spare me or destroy me as thou pleasest. I would rather be eaten by such a noble animal as thou art than by wolves and jackals." Thus replied the goat, with the resourcefulness of one suddenly confronted with danger.

Pleased with the goat's flattery, the noble beast spared his life, and, biting off one of his ivory-like crescent-shaped claws, gave it to him as his passport through the forest of which he was the king. "Keep this with thee," quoth he, "and, if thou art attacked by any one of my subject-beasts, just hold it up before him, and he shall leave thee harmless." With that, away he bounded into the darkness.

Now that he was armed with this passport, the goat decided to stay where he was until day-break. With the first streaks of light he rose, and, after a long tramp, found a path which brought him safely out of the wood. He was by this time overcome with hunger and thirst, and so, seeing a beautifully laid-out park, with here and there a fountain, and ablaze with many-coloured blossoms, he walked straight into it and was soon regaling himself with the honeyed flowers. Now this park belonged to a Prince, and the gardener, finding an ownerless goat damaging the flowers, seized him and took him before his royal master, who demanded of the goat in haughty tones, "Why hast thou damaged my park? Tell me who thy master is."

"I belong to a royal flock," whined the goat. "Misfortune has separated me from my companions. I ate up thy flowers because I was hungry, and hunger knows no law. Now do as thou pleasest with me."

The Prince, somewhat pacified, again enquired of the goat who his master was and where he lived, but the goat would not enlighten him on either point.

Since, however, the goat belonged to a fellow-prince, he gave him permission to remain in his kingdom until his royal owner could be discovered, and directed him to go and graze in the forest instead of in his park.

"O Prince," replied the goat, prostrating himself to the ground before him, and almost digging his horns into his feet in the process, "I dare not go into the forest to graze, for there I am sure to be eaten up by tigers or wolves."

The Prince had not thought of this, and felt the force of the goat's objection. "Yes, thou art right," said the Prince, after a moment's thought, "I never dreamt of that; thou art the property of a brother Prince and must be taken every care of until such time as he can be found." So saying, he ordered one of his elephants to take the goat into the forest on his back and feed him on grass and twigs plucked with his trunk; and thus the goat had delightful rides every day and throve well, as you may imagine.

It soon happened that the elephant whose duty it was to carry the goat about came to be ridiculed by other elephants for bearing such a mean burden, while they themselves, adorned with gold and silver trappings, had the honour of carrying no less a being than the Prince himself.

Stung to the quick by these taunts, the elephant went before his royal master and, kneeling down, spake thus: "O Prince, what has thy servant done that thou shouldest make him, who has hitherto borne no other being than thyself, carry such a mean thing as a goat on his back? Do thou permit me to take him across the forest to the country from whence he came, and make him over to his owner."

"Very well," replied the Prince, and the goat departed for his country.

The elephant, once across the forest, had no difficulty in tracing out the country from which the goat had come, and, putting him down before his royal master, said: "O Prince, here is thy truant goat who trespassed into the kingdom of my master, a Prince like unto thyself, and he commissioned me to deliver him into thy hands."

Thus saying, the elephant was about to turn back, when the goat, addressing the Prince, said: "O Prince, allow me to go back with the elephant to my new master, who has taken better care of me, as thou mayst judge by my appearance, than thou ever didst before. I do not desire to live in thy kingdom."

When the Prince heard this, he turned to the elephant and said: "Take back this ungrateful wretch. I will have none of him;" and the elephant seized him by his hind legs, swung him on to his back, and departed.

While nearing his country, the elephant had to cross a rivulet and, in doing so, pitched the goat right into it. The goat swam across as best he could, and, when he got over to the other side, he was quite exhausted, and had moreover lost the passport given him by the lion. He ran after the elephant, bleating, and in this way both came into the presence of the Prince.

The elephant then narrated to the Prince all that had passed between the goat and his royal master, and the Prince, when he had heard the whole story, banished the ungrateful goat from his kingdom, just as his own master had done.

Thus driven from pillar to post, the goat soon found himself back in the mazes of the dreaded forest, but this time his wits failed him in the hour of danger, and his plump body was soon shared between wolves and jackals.

THE ELEPHANT-WRESTLER.

ONCE upon a time there lived a poor old widow with a grown-up son, who, though not a giant, was yet endowed with a giant's strength. Their only means of livelihood was the making and selling of pots of clay. These they used to leave in front of their hut, to be sun-dried previous to being baked in a kiln.

It so happened, one day, that the King of the land, who was going out to hunt on an elephant, passed by their hut, and the elephant crushed under its heavy feet the pots which were lying about in the sun. The widow's son, seeing this, rushed up from behind and caught hold of the tail of the elephant, which suddenly stopped and, in spite of the goading of the driver, could not be made to move at all. Mad with pain, it began to bellow and whirl its trunk about, almost shaking the Prince off its back. Looking behind, the Prince was surprised to see a mere youth clinging to the elephant's tail with all his might.

"Why dost thou hold up my elephant, O foolish youth?" thundered the Prince.

"I am, O Prince, a poor subject of thine and live by pottery," replied the youth, apologetically. "Dost thou not see, O Prince, the damage done to my pots by thy elephant?"

"Is that why thou clingest to my elephant, Mr. Elephant-wrestler?" said the King. "Come to me when I return from the hunt, and thou shalt get gold for thy clay."

The youth thanked his sovereign and let go his hold of the tail of the elephant.

The following day, when the King returned home, the Elephant-wrestler, as the youth had now come to be known, waited upon him at the palace.

"Is it thou, Mr. Elephant-wrestler?" said the King. "Didst thou not commit an act of treason against thy sovereign by holding up his elephant yesterday? Well," the King went on, flinging a purse of money towards him, "this purse will more than compensate thee for all the damage done to thy pottery, but thou must at once depart from my kingdom."

The Elephant-wrestler now returned home to his old mother, and putting the money into her hands said: "Mother, I have been banished from the kingdom, but never mind, thou shalt not feel the want of money. This purse contains enough to last the few remaining years of thy life."

Thus saying, he departed from his native land as an exile, but his fame for physical strength, and therewith his nickname of Elephant-wrestler, came to be more and more widely known with every revolving moon.

He journeyed on and on, not caring whither, and, as he tramped along, he came across a youth crushing coin after coin to powder between thumb and forefinger. "Who art thou?" asked the Elephant-wrestler of him.

"I am," said the youth, "a pupil of the Elephant-wrestler."

"And I am that same Elephant-wrestler," replied the Elephant-wrestler, not a little surprised.

"If thou art indeed the Elephant-wrestler," said the youth, "I must serve thee, so take me with thee wherever thou goest."

"Very well; come with me," replied the Elephant-wrestler.

Thus was the Elephant-wrestler joined by the youth, and, before they had gone very far, they met another youth pulling trees up by the roots as he went along.

"Who art thou, O stranger?" asked the Elephant-wrestler of him.

"I am," said the second youth, "a pupil of the Elephant-wrestler."

"Know me, then," replied the latter, "to be the Elephant-wrestler you speak of."

"If thou art indeed he," said the youth, "let me, as a favour, accompany thee wherever thou goest."

"So be it; the more the merrier," was the reply, and he too joined the Elephant-wrestler.

The party of three then went along merrily together until they came to a river which stood in the way of their further progress, and there was no boat to take them across. In this predicament, the Elephant-wrestler ordered his pupils to jump right across to the other side.

"We are afraid," said the youths; "the task is quite beyond our powers."

Thereupon the Elephant-wrestler seized them both, one by the left hand and the other by the right, and flung them across with the greatest ease. After that, he jumped right over the river himself, as if he were jumping over a fence, and, as luck or ill-luck would have it, a big fish leaped ashore immediately after him. He caught it up as he would have caught a foot-ball, and, hungry as he was, he told one of his pupils to dress it for cooking and sent the other away to get from somewhere a fire with which to cook it. The latter went about in quest of fuel, and at last found himself in what appeared to be a deserted city. To his surprise no human being met his eyes; but, as he was about to retrace his steps in disappointment, a withered old woman, bent and double with age, came hobbling along towards him on a crutch.

"Who art thou, and what has brought thee hither?" asked the aged crone of the youth.

"I am a pupil of the world-famous Elephant-wrestler, come to beg for fuel," said the youth.

"Very well; come with me to my hut, and thou shalt have it," said the old hag to him.

Suspecting nothing, the youth followed her to her hut, when lo! she suddenly turned into a huge giantess, and, opening wide her mouth, swallowed him up.

A long while elapsed, and, as the youth had not returned, the Elephant-wrestler, impatient of delay, sent his other pupil away to look for him and fetch materials for the fire.

He, too, wandered into the deserted city and met the same fate as his companion at the hands of the ogress.

When neither of the pupils returned, the Elephant-wrestler became alarmed, and, burying the fish in the sands, went to look for them. He too followed the same route as his two pupils had taken, and at last came across the ogress hobbling along on her crutch.

"Hast thou seen, O woman," asked the Elephant-wrestler when she came near, "any of my pupils about here?"

"I do not know who are thy pupils," replied the ogress, "but two youths asked me for fire, and said they would like to have a look round at the city before calling for it. Come with me to my hut, and when they come back thou wilt know who they are."

The Elephant-wrestler accompanied her to her hut, and no sooner had he arrived there than the old woman assumed a gigantic form and opened wide her mouth to swallow him up. He quickly guessed who she was and what had become of his pupils, and, without a moment's delay, struck her a heavy blow on each of her cheeks. At this, the ogress opened wide her jaws in pain, and, lo! out popped his two pupils through the crater-like cavity of her mouth.

Now the Elephant-wrestler and his pupils showered blows fast and furious upon her, and at every blow she disgorged men, women, and children whom she had swallowed. Last of all, out came the King and Queen of the land, with all their ministers and courtiers, and the deserted city once more became populous.

Not content with this achievement, the Elephant-wrestler leapt, sword in hand, into the mouth of the ogress, and, after having thoroughly examined her inside, got himself out by cutting her open. Thus perished the ogress.

Now the King, out of gratitude, begged the Elephant-wrestler to live in his kingdom in luxury, but he refused to lead a life of inglorious ease. At the request of the King, however, he left with him one of his pupils to guard his kingdom against any future foes. He then took his departure, accompanied by his other pupil, and loaded with costly presents. Before parting, he gave his pupil one of his swords, saying: "O my dear pupil, keep this sword carefully. If thou ever seest blood exude from it, then know me to be in danger and come to my assistance, if thou carest."

He now went on in the company of his pupil, meeting with many adventures on his way, one of which so far exceeded the others in bravery that it deserves to be told.

It so happened that one night the two travellers came to the outskirts of a walled city, close to which they heard the growls of tigers. Here they selected a spot in which to encamp, and went to sleep by turns. The pupil first laid down to sleep, while the Elephant-wrestler kept watch over him. Soon the tigers appeared and made a fierce attack, but the Elephant-wrestler killed every one of them with his club with as much ease as if he were destroying rats. Just then his pupil awoke, and it was the Elephant-wrestler's turn to sleep. Shortly afterwards the remainder of the tigers appeared and were similarly dealt with by the brave youth.

Next morning, as the King was going out of the city to hunt, he was surprised to see two men lying on a bed of tigers. When he heard what had happened, he was so pleased with the extirpation of these pests, which had been making havoc among his subjects for many years, that he invited the Elephant-wrestler and his pupil to live in his kingdom in luxury for the rest of their mortal lives, but the Elephant-wrestler again refused to lead a life of inglorious ease. So at last, at the King's request, he left with him his remaining pupil, to whom he also gave a sword, saying: "O my dear pupil, keep this sword carefully. If thou seest blood exude from it, then know me to be in danger and come to my assistance, if thou carest."

In spite of having been banished, he now departed for his native land, loaded with costly gifts, to see his mother. As soon as the news of his arrival came to the ears of his sovereign, he sent several armed men to arrest him and bring him before him for punishment, but the Elephant-wrestler hit right and left and killed each and every one of them. At last the King was compelled to send a whole army against him, and this time succeeded in arresting him. As he was now in danger, blood began to exude from the swords which he had given to his pupils, who speedily came to his assistance, each with a huge army, and restored him to liberty.

The King, now pleased with the Elephant-wrestler, gave him his daughter in marriage, and half his kingdom for dower, and the two lived happily ever after.

UNCLE TIGER.

ONCE upon a time, by a wood, two brothers dwelt with their wives under their father's roof. For in the olden days, when the family was all-in-all and the individual was of small account, it was not unusual for several generations to live together under a common head. Frequently, however, such a family suffered from discord and jealousy among its members, especially among its womenfolk; and so it was that quarrels between the wives of the two brothers had often occurred. The wife of the elder brother was the evil genius of the family, and hated her sister-in-law because, forsooth, she was handsomer than herself.

So spiteful was her conduct towards her sister-in-law, that the latter's life became quite unbearable. Matters became worse and worse, until at last one evening the poor woman stole out into the wood, and, sitting down on a boulder on the bank of a stream, began to bewail her lot. A tiger chanced to come to the stream to drink water, and, being moved to pity by her cries, (for beauty in tears is said to turn away even the fierceness of wild beasts), enquired the reason of her unhappiness.

"Uncle Tiger," replied the woman, resigned to any fate, "I am so unhappy at home. Take me away with thee to thy den, and I will serve thee and thy wife, and tend thy cubs."

"My dear niece," said the tiger, "thou art welcome to my den, and I will see to it that thou shalt want nothing to make thee happy, but I know not how thou wouldst like tigers for thy companions. How dost thou like my face?" he asked her after a pause.

"Why," she said, so as to humour him, "it is as beautiful as a full moon."

"What dost thou think of my tail?" asked the tiger, smiling.

"Oh," replied his niece, "it is as beautiful as the rainbow."

"How do I smell?" asked the tiger again, evidently pleased with her answers. Of course, the odour was nauseating in the extreme, but she continued to play her part well, and said: "Thy smell? Why, it is as sweet as that of sandal-wood paste."

Highly pleased with replies so flattering to his vanity, Uncle Tiger now took her away to his den. On the way they met with other tigers, who, seeing her in the company of one of their kind, fancied she was intended to provide a feast for them, and began to follow her; but her companion drove them off with a growl.

Arrived at the den, the tiger introduced her to his mate, and the care of their young ones was entrusted to her.

Every day she used to keep guard over the cubs, and play with them while their parents went out in search of food, and thus passed her days away in a round of unvaried routine, until the time came when she felt a longing to be at home again.

Uncle Tiger and Aunt Tigress were much pleased with her faithful services, so they determined not to let her depart without bestowing valuable gifts upon her, and so it came about that Uncle Tiger made a raid one day upon a jeweller's shop and carried away all the jewellery he could lay his paws on for his niece, while Aunt Tigress plundered a silk shop and succeeded in bringing away a large quantity of rich silk. Similar visits to other shops followed. When they had collected all their plentiful booty, they made an army of bears carry it on their heads, human fashion, while they themselves offered to escort their niece, dressed in a flowing silk robe and sparkling with jewellery, through the jungle to her home.

Whilst everybody but her wicked sister-in-law was rending the air with lamentations, she suddenly appeared in her rustling silk robes and sparkling jewels, with the tiger and tigress on either side of her, followed by the bears carrying trays of valuable gifts on their heads.

At once the lamentations ceased, and there was an attempt at a general stampede among the inmates ; but, rushing forward, she dispelled their fears, and introduced Uncle Tiger and Aunt Tigress to them, telling them how kind they had been to her, and how they had escorted her home with bear-loads of gifts. Confidence having been fully restored, the tigers and bears were sumptuously fed ere they departed to the wood, and, when they were leaving, Uncle Tiger and Aunt Tigress promised to look in again and enquire after their niece.

The wife of her brother-in-law now envied her lot, and, wishing to get rich as speedily as her sister-in-law had done, betook herself one evening to the wood, and, sitting down on the bank of the stream, kept saying aloud : "Uncle Tiger ! take me away to thy den. Uncle Tiger ! take me away to thy den."

As it happened the very tiger which had befriended her sister-in-law passed at that moment on his way to see his niece, and, hearing his name uttered, ran up to her and enquired why she was calling him.

"Oh, Uncle Tiger, I am so unhappy at home," cried the woman. "Do thou take me away to thy den, where I will serve thee and thy wife."

Uncle Tiger, however, felt sceptical about her desire to share his den with him, and, being anxious to find out whether she would really like to have tigers as companions, he asked her what his face was like.

"Thy face, Uncle Tiger?" replied the woman, laughing. "Why, it is like that of a jungle cat, only many times bigger."

"And what dost thou think of my tail?" asked the tiger, frowning.

"Thy tail, Uncle Tiger? It is as handsome as a monkey's, only much stouter and larger," was the reply.

"And my dear niece," said the tiger, grinding his teeth audibly, "hast thou got anything to say about my smell?"

"Thy smell, Uncle Tiger?" replied the unsuspecting woman, taking out her handkerchief and putting it to her nose. "Oh, it has passed into a byword with us. If anything smells abominably, as thou dost, we say it is like a tiger. Thou dost not know how thou smellest, Uncle Tiger?" she added with a provocative laugh.

Of course the tiger was incensed by what the woman had said about him, and, mad with anger, he flew at her, and, ripping open her face with his claws, let her go home uglier than she was before. Thus was her jealousy cured for all time, and peace again prevailed in the family.

THE CRAB PRINCE.

ONCE upon a time a poor lone widow, suddenly deprived of the roof over her head by a storm, knew not where to find shelter for herself, so, being forced to beg, she wandered about looking for a deserted hut. One she came upon had evidently at one time been the home of a family of fisher folks. This hut, which stood by the river-side, was deserted save for one occupant, a vermilion-coloured crab, and, strange to say, the woman got quite fond of this creature, which soon returned her affection and used to call her mother.

They were indeed strange companions, and one evening, while the woman sat at her door with the crab in her lap, she said: "Thou callest me mother, O crab! but thou canst not relieve my distress as a son of my womb would do."

"O mother," replied the crab, somewhat moved, "thou needst not go a-begging. I will bring thee on the morrow enough of everything to last the remainder of thy life; so cheer up and sweep thy floor clean."

The woman got up, pleased with the crab, and swept the hut clean.

Next morning the crab went out and first visited a wheat shop. "Brother, wilt thou sell me as much wheat as I can carry in both my ears?" said the crab to the shop-keeper.

"Hullo, Crabby!" replied the latter, highly amused, "thou canst help thyself to as much corn as thou canst carry in thine ears. I make a gift of it to thee."

So, while the shop-keeper was otherwise engaged, the crab crammed his ears full of the corn and walked coolly away. He returned to his hut and poured out the corn upon the floor in a heap, and out he went again. In like manner he visited shop after shop, and carried away enough of everything to last him and his mother for many and many a long day.

The crab then said to the old woman: "O mother dear, can I not relieve thy distress? Thou must henceforth look upon me as if thou hadst borne me."

The woman was overjoyed at this turn of fortune and began to live happily. Yet she had still one more complaint to make to her son, and that was about their tumble-down hut.

Out went the crab again, and, going up to a money-lender, asked for a loan of money.

"Hullo, Crabby!" said the money-lender, amused at such a request proceeding from a crab, "thou needest money, dost thou?" and with that he threw a quantity of gold coins towards him. "Take these away, if thou canst carry them, as a free gift from me," said the money-lender, and lo! in the twinkling of an eye, the crab safely stowed away all these coins in his ears and walked quietly away, to the amazement of everybody.

With this money he built a mansion where the hut had formerly stood, and the crab and his mother continued to live happily together.

There are no bounds, however, to the vanity of human wishes. At last came a day when the widow let drop a tear upon the crab, as she sat fondling him.

"Why dost thou weep, mother dear?" said the crab. "What is the matter? Is there anything else wanting to make thee happy? Tell me, and thy will shall be done."

"O my dear son, thou hast done more than a son could have done for me, yet if thou hadst been a man thou mightest marry and bring a charming bride into this mansion, and thy children would play round my knees and prattle to me."

"Is that all? Thou shalt have a Princess for thy daughter-in-law, I warrant thee. I will wed no commoner; so dry thy tears and cheer up, O mother dear."

So the woman rose, dreaming of a daughter-in-law, and went about her household work with a light heart, while the crab made for the palace of the King of the land, to seek for the hand of his daughter.

On the way he was accosted by a cat. "Whither art thou going, brother crab?" asked the cat.

"I am going to wed the King's daughter," replied the crab.

"Let me go with thee to thy wedding, brother," prayed the cat.

"Slip into my ear," said the crab, and the cat did as he was bid. He went along and next met with a tiger. "Whither art thou going, brother crab?" asked the tiger.

"I am going to wed the King's daughter," replied the crab.

"I long to taste thy wedding cake. Take me along with thee," implored the tiger.

"Slip into my ear, brother tiger," said the crab, and the tiger did as he was bid.

Next the crab came to a clump of bamboos not far from the palace.

"Whither art thou going, brother crab?" asked the bamboos.

"I am going to wed the King's daughter," replied the crab.

"Do not leave us behind. We want to witness thy wedding," prayed the bamboos.

"Slip into my ear," said the crab, and they did as they were bid.

Thus did the crab continue his journey until he came to a river.

"Whither art thou going, brother crab?" asked the river.

"I am going to wed the King's daughter," replied the crab.

"Let me go to thy wedding, brother crab," pleaded the river.

"Slip into my ear," said the crab, and the river did as she was bid.

At last he arrived at the palace and kept saying aloud: "O Prince! make me thy son-in-law. O Prince! make me thy son-in-law."

The Prince ordered one of his pages to seize the crab and bring him before him, but, when the page laid his hand upon the crab, the latter snipped his fingers off with his sharp claws. Dropping him like a hot cake, the page, bleeding and crying, ran back to the Prince, who gave orders to have the crab caught and brought up for punishment. This being done, the Prince addressed him:

"Dost thou dare ask for the hand of my daughter, thou saucy crab? I will torture thee and put thee to death." And, so saying, the Prince ordered the crab to be shut up with his fighting-cocks so that they might riddle him through and through with their beaks and claws.

This was done, but, when the cocks began to attack the crab, out came the cat, who, after killing and eating them, slipped back into his ear.

Next morning the Prince was surprised to find the crab unharmed and heaps of feathers in place of the cocks.

Flying into a rage, he ordered the crab to be tied by all his ten legs to the pillar-like leg of a huge elephant, so that he might be crushed to death under his heavy feet.

This was done, and out came the tiger from his hiding-place and killed the elephant, after which he unbound the crab and slipped back into his ear.

Next morning, when the King went to see what had happened to the crab, great was his amazement to find one of his finest elephants lying dead upon the ground.

He next ordered a number of soldiers to kill the crab, and, when they came to seize him, out came the bamboos, which began to belabour them mercilessly until they embraced the earth one by one.

The anger of the King now knew no bounds. Not knowing how to get rid of the crab, he had him tied to one of the legs of his bedstead for the night, and lo! when the King was asleep, the river flowed out of the crab's ear, and away floated the bedstead. When the King awoke from his sleep and found himself on the point of drowning, he made his peace with the crab by promising to give him his daughter for a wife, if only he would recall the river into his ear.

The crab then bound the King by a three-fold oath, and immediately the river slipped back into his ear.

The crab was soon wedded to the King's daughter, amidst more sorrow than joy, as one might have expected, and after the wedding the bridegroom returned home with his royal bride in grand procession.

The widow, his mother, was now beside herself with joy, and welcomed the bride. Thus was her heart's desire fulfilled.

The King, curious to know how his daughter was getting on with her crab husband, paid a visit to her, and was surprised to find her anything but unhappy. The secret was now revealed to the King. The crab was a crab by day, but a Prince by night.

At the suggestion of the King, while her husband was asleep, the Princess had his shell pounded to dust, and so, on getting up from bed, he missed his shell and could no more disguise himself. There was now rejoicing at the palace, where before there had been beating of breasts and tearing of hair.

THE GIANT OUTWITTED BY THE DWARF.

ONCE upon a time there was a merchant who lived in great opulence until a giant came and took up his quarters in the neighbourhood, and then his star began to set.

The giant ate up all his neighbours, one by one, and last of all the merchant himself; but by sheer good luck his wife, with their little child, a dwarf, escaped destruction, having been absent on a visit to her brother.

After having devoured the merchant, the giant transferred his residence to his mansion, and continued to live there unmolested, as if he were "monarch of all he surveyed," while the merchant's widow became dependent upon her brother.

The child, a bright little dwarf, grew up under his uncle's care and began to play with companions of his own age.

On one occasion, his playmates taunted him with living on his uncle, and the boy ran home weeping to his mother and told her what had been said to him.

"My dear boy," said the mother, "thy father was a wealthy merchant, but a wicked giant came and ate him up and now rules in our house. So long as he lives, we cannot go back to it and come by our own."

After this, the dwarf, who used to help his mother in the kitchen, presented himself before the giant and prayed to be made his cook.

"What?" cried the giant. "Thou darest to walk into a lion's den? I am a giant and will make a meal of thee."

"Oh, do not kill me, Sir Giant," pleaded the boy, with folded hands. "I am too small to provide a meal for thee, but, if thou shouldest spare my life, I will cook thee nice dishes every day."

"Very well," said the giant, after a moment's reflection. "I could swallow up at a gulp a dozen such little dwarfs as thou art and yet would go hungry. So I agree to thy proposal, but, should thy cooking be not to my taste, thou shalt die."

The boy became his cook on these terms of life and death, and the dainty dishes prepared by him were such as the giant had never tasted before.

Thus the dwarf lived with the giant.

Every day after breakfast, the giant used to go out, returning home at dinner time.

One day the boy gathered up sufficient courage to ask his master whither he was in the habit of going.

"What matter to thee my goings out and comings in?" replied the giant.

"I do not mean to pry into thy business, Sir Giant," whined the boy, "but, if I know where thou goest every day, I can so time my cooking as to be able to serve thee thy dinner hot from the oven."

"I am Clerk to the God of Destiny," replied the Giant, unthinkingly, "and my only business is to register his decrees and, conformably thereto, measure out and allot unto mortals their spans of existence on earth."

"Wilt thou be pleased, Sir Giant," said the boy, "to ask thy master, the God of Destiny, what is the period of life allotted unto me?"

When the giant next returned home, the dwarf asked him what the God of Destiny had told him in answer to his query.

"The God said thou shalt live a full century," replied the giant.

"Wilt thou be pleased, Sir Giant, to ask him on the morrow," said the boy, "if he can reduce my allotted span of life by so much as a fraction of a fraction of a second?"

Next day, when the giant returned home hungry, the dwarf wanted to know what his master, the God of Destiny, had said as to that, and the giant thus replied: "The God said no one can meddle with the span of life allotted unto thee. Thou shalt live a full century, neither a second more nor a second less."

The dwarf now ran into the kitchen and, instead of bringing the giant his dinner, took up a burning faggot and ran towards him, saying: "What? Since no one can take away my life before its time, why should I be afraid of thee any more?"

The giant, thus outwitted by the dwarf, and thinking discretion the better part of valour, took to his heels.

The dwarf and his mother now recovered their house, and one by one their old neighbours returned, and never more was the giant seen.

THE HIRELING HUSBAND.

ONCE upon a time there was a proud and haughty monarch, and in his pride he neglected the gods and feared them not. He had married seven Queens, and each of them had borne him a son. "What a joy to have such a family!" said he to himself, as he beheld his seven grown-up sons around him. "I own extensive dominions, and would rather trust my sons to govern them for me than even the most trustworthy among my ministers."

Filled with such thoughts, the King called his seven sons, and, intending to let them govern such of his possessions as their gratitude and affection for him should seem to deserve, said to them one by one: "My dear son, who feeds thee and cares for thee?"

"Why, father," said the six oldest sons, "who else should feed and care for us but thou? Has any of us been so ungrateful as to have denied that?"

"No," replied the King; "I was only thinking of making you governors of my provinces, and so, to know from your own lips which of you loved me best and were most grateful to me, so as to deserve my trust, I put the question to each of you. I am pleased with your answers and appoint you each a governor of one province."

When the turn of the youngest Prince came to answer the question, he bluntly said: "What a queer question to put? Father, who else can feed me but my own good destiny? 'What's lotted can't be blotted.'"

The King flew into a great fury and banished him then and there from his kingdom, saying: "Oh, thou ungrateful wretch, if thy good destiny feeds thee, look to it to feed thee in thy exile. Thou art henceforth no son of mine."

Thus banished, the Prince bowed to his father and went away to seek his fortune elsewhere. He journeyed on and on, not knowing whither, until chance brought him to another kingdom. According to the laws of this country, every foreigner found therein had to be brought before the King, and only when he was found to be of good character was he ever allowed to stay. So no sooner had the Prince arrived there than he was seized and straightway taken before the King, who immediately took a fancy to him on account of his handsome appearance, and chose him to be companion to his son, a one-eyed Prince of equal age with him.

Thus did his good destiny befriend him in his darkest hour of trial.

As time went on, the father of the one-eyed Prince thought of getting his son married, but, as he was blind of one eye, none of the Princesses around cared to be his wife; at last necessity, which is said to be the mother of invention, suggested an ingenious way out of the difficulty.

"Why not get my son married by proxy?" said the King to himself. "Why not let his companion, who is of the same age as he is and not a whit less handsome, play the bridegroom on his behalf, going through the marriage in his name, but letting him into the bridal chamber by stealth directly after the nuptials ? "

And so, having thought out his plan, he proceeded to put it into action by sending out match-makers in every direction. It happened that another King, who had a grown-up Princess to marry, had, by a curious coincidence, similarly sent out a match-maker to look out for a bridegroom, and that he, having wandered far and wide without success, at last arrived at this kingdom quite exhausted and worn out. He soon discovered the son of the King to have but one eye, yet, having become too fatigued to go elsewhere to seek for a better bridegroom, he struck a bargain with the King then and there, promising to keep his tongue between his teeth as regarded his son's blindness.

Loaded with rewards, he returned to his master, told him how he had settled the marriage of the Princess with a remarkably handsome Prince, and thus received fresh rewards for his pains.

The wedding-day came, and the Prince's companion, dressed as a bridegroom, started in grand procession for the house of the bride, in company with the King and his one-eyed son.

Arrived there, the sham Prince and his party were received in right royal style with every circumstance of pomp and grandeur. Everyone at the palace was captivated by the sweet manners and handsome appearance of the bridegroom, and the wedding passed off without a hitch. Immediately after the marriage, however, the bridegroom, according to his compact with his master, stole out of the bridal-chamber and rejoined his own party.

The Princess, missing him from her chamber, sent out her maid to look for him amongst the men of his party, and, sure enough, there she found him. After some persuasion she induced him to return with her to the Princess. On the way back, however, the Princess, who feared he might again leave her, had caused artificial tigers, bears, and lions to be set up. As soon as the Prince and the maid had crossed the road where these pretended beasts were concealed, they suddenly came in view, looking as fierce and threatening as if they had been alive.

The maid, pretending to be greatly alarmed, begged the Prince to hurry up as there were wild beasts behind them, and pointed to the sham tigers, bears, and lions with her finger; but the Prince, who knew not fear, offered to go back and kill them all with his sword. As that would have spoilt her plans, she entreated him to quicken his steps, saying she would fall down in a swoon if he tarried. The chivalrous Prince had to comply with her entreaties.

Thus was the wandering sheep brought back into the fold again, and, when the Princess saw her bridegroom, she took him to task for having run away from her, but soon she made it up with him and begged him to play a game of chance, before retiring, just to ascertain, she pleaded, how their married life would fare.

The Prince, to whom nothing came amiss, agreed to her request. While they were engaged in play, the Princess began to doze, and at last fell asleep, and the Prince, taking advantage of this, wrote in golden characters on the hem of her flowing robe his name and pedigree and the curious history of the marriage, and then decamped for good.

When the Princess awoke, it was daylight, and the bridegroom was not at her side. She consoled herself with thinking that he must have gone back to his friends among the men of his party, and, when night came on, he told her maid to go and fetch him as she had done the night before.

Now the one-eyed Prince, who had put on the dress of his proxy and was wearing a big turban which came down over the blind eye, almost concealing it, met the maid and accompanied her to the Princess. On the way back they had to pass the same fierce-looking artificial beasts, and the maid entreated him to quicken his steps, as she pretended the animals were after them. No sooner had the one-eyed Prince looked behind and seen the beasts, than he began to quake all over through fright, and only kept himself from falling down in a swoon by catching hold of the maid, who screamed out and shook him off with much difficulty.

Arrived at the palace, the counterfeit bridegroom walked into the chamber, trembling with fear as if he had been suddenly seized with ague. The maid narrated to her mistress all that had happened on the way, wondering in her own mind whether he was really the bridegroom, for his behaviour had been so strange and unlike that of a Prince. However, the Princess had seen her bridegroom only for a short time, and so, to find out beyond all possibility of doubt, whether the gaudily-dressed young man before her was really her wedded husband, she asked him to play a game of chance with her. To her surprise he professed total ignorance of all games, and could not remember a single word of their talk on the wedding night. Suddenly the Princess noticed one of his eyes all but hidden by the turban, which she lifted up, when lo! she found him blind of one eye and had him instantly turned out of her chamber, neck and crop.

The one-eyed Prince ran back, weeping, to his father and told him of his woes. Finding that the fraud had been discovered, the King in great dismay beat a hasty retreat from the country.

In the meantime the Princess was at a loss what to do, not knowing who her husband was nor where he lived. In the end she could do nothing but keep her soul in patience in the hope of his some day returning to claim his bride.

In spring, when the earth is gay with flowers, and the birds fill the air with sound, the swinging carnival is held, and so it happened that the Princess put on her wedding garment and started swinging with her companions, when lo! the end of her robe swept the ground before her, and the golden letters recording the name and pedigree of her husband shone out in the sun. She quickly jumped down from the swing and learnt for the first time who her husband was and where he lived.

Overjoyed with the discovery, she ran straight to her father and thus said to him: "O father, the home of a married woman, be she a Princess or a commoner, should always be where her husband's home is. I am determined to go in search of my husband, so wilt thou be pleased to give me an army for my protection?"

The King tried to dissuade her from her purpose, pointing out the difficulty of the task, but she was not to be moved from her resolve. At last the King had no alternative but to give her an army consisting of his bravest and most trusted soldiers, and, dressing herself in a man's clothes, the Princess set off on her travels.

The first thing she did was to go to the kingdom of her husband's father, and besiege it, challenging her father-in-law to give her battle; but the old King, not desiring bloodshed and fearing defeat, submitted to her, and was compelled to produce and give up his youngest Prince to her as a hostage. After that, she threw off her disguise as a Prince and declared herself to be the bride of his youngest son.

The King now realized the truth of what his youngest son had said to him, and, flinging himself upon his neck, said: "My dear son, thou didst speak the truth. 'What is lotted can't be blotted.' Thy bride has won my kingdom for thee, and it is no longer mine to give away."

From that time forward, the Prince and Princess lived happily together and ruled their people well and wisely.